The Power of Pause: Mastering Delayed Gratification for Success

First printing May 2024

Library of Congress Cataloging-in-Publication Data

Justo, M.D., Emilio M.
The Power of Pause: Mastering Delayed Gratification for Success / by Emilio M. Justo, M.D.

Paperback ISBN: 978-1-965092-19-4
Hardcover ISBN: 978-1-965092-20-0
Dustjacket ISBN: 978-1-965092-21-7

Published by AR PRESS, an American Real Publishing Company
Roger L. Brooks, Publisher
roger@incubatemedia.us
americanrealpublishing.com

Edited by: Katie Ressa
Interior design by Eva Myrick, MSCP

Printed in the U.S.A.

THE POWER OF PAUSE:
Mastering Delayed Gratification for Success

A BLUEPRINT FOR RESILIENCE AND ENDURING FULFILLMENT

EMILIO M. JUSTO, M.D.

In *The Power of Pause*, Dr. Emilio Justo offers a compelling narrative of resilience and success through the lens of delayed gratification. His personal story shines through as the ideal step-by-step process for anyone to reach their highest goals. Dr. Justo's insights serve as a compelling blueprint for personal growth, resilience, and fulfillment, making this book a must-read for those seeking profound transformation.

—Will Harris
CEO | Willpower Consultation

I have struggled for years with delaying gratification. Personally, I enjoy having and eating my cake immediately. I know it truly has hindered my ability to be resilient and anytime I have delayed gratification in an area, the reward was sweeter and everything ultimately flowed more effortlessly. The challenge is that I didn't have an actual blueprint for how to really delay gratification or anything that demonstrated why it was important to do so—until now. This book has the power to change many lives. Buy it. Read it. Ear mark it —and prepare for the new life to follow.

—Corey Poirier
Multiple-Time TEDx Speaker
bLU Talks Founder
Wall Street Journal/USA Today Bestselling Author

The Power of Pause provides not just the idea of delayed gratification but helpful "how-tos" that make the book special. Dr. Justo has not only put his finger on a critical component needed in our lives, but helps us make the changes necessary to gain this "superpower." In a world that loves instant everything, this book is a breath of fresh air that promises more than a quick fix or a top five list and gets to the core of how we can embrace delayed gratification and lean into the power that the pause brings.

—**Bob Fabey**
International Speaker and
Business Consultant at Fabey Insights

This book provides vital insight into the value of delaying gratification to seek a deeper, longer-lasting reward. Dr. Justo provides the vital tools for how to strategically plan choices centered around enduring happiness and true-life successes. Any reader will walk away with keys to ensuring they can accomplish the goals they would like to walk a path of a healthy and meaningful existence.

—**Yarona Boster**
Communications Master
Advanced Certified Life Coach
Certified Speaker Coach

Foreword

In an era characterized by the relentless pursuit of immediate satisfaction, where the digital world has drastically shortened our attention spans and amplified our desires for instant rewards, *The Power of Pause: Mastering Delayed Gratification for Success* emerges not just as a book, but as a vital counter-narrative to societal norms.

Emilio M. Justo, M.D. invites his readers on an introspective journey, challenging us to recalibrate our internal compasses and align our actions with our most profound aspirations. It is an exploration into the art of delayed gratification—an admitted newfound skill for me that, once mastered, promises to unlock unparalleled levels of personal and professional achievement.

Delayed gratification, the cornerstone upon which this book is built, is a concept deeply rooted in our psychological makeup. In an American culture that values speed over depth, and immediate pleasure over lasting fulfillment, this philosophical approach is not only increasingly overlooked—it is ignored. Through a meticulously curated blend of a lifetime of practice and research, philosophical insights, and transformative real-life stories, this book sheds light on how the intentional act of pausing can serve as a powerful catalyst for growth. In essence, it's a place where instant gratification goes back to school and into a "retoolment" period, whereby it resurfaces to the world in an entirely new way.

As you immerse yourself in the pages that follow, you will encounter a rich narrative written by an eye surgeon who has reached the pinnacle of success by steadfastly adhering to his core principles of delayed gratification, providing compelling evidence that illustrates the far-reaching benefits of this unique practice. His real-life experiences underscore the profound impact that waiting, planning, and persevering can have on our personal growth, careers and most importantly, our lives.

Beyond its exploration of the theoretical underpinnings of delayed gratification, "The Power of Pause" is rich in context with practical strategies and approaches designed to help readers cultivate patience, build resilience, and achieve a more balanced and fulfilling life. The book offers a blueprint for navigating the temptations of immediate satisfaction, providing readers with concepts to assess the long-term implications of their choices and to prioritize actions that align with their ultimate goals.

Above all, what truly sets this book apart is its timely message—a sensible call to reclaim the lost art of patience in a world increasingly defined by the desire for immediate results. It serves as a reminder that true success is seldom a product of haste; rather, it is the outcome of thoughtful decision-making, strategic planning, and the willingness to embrace the journey, with all its delays and detours, as part of the path to achieving our most intimate desires.

Being a fellow traveler with you on this path, I extend an invitation for you to pause, to ponder, and to embrace the transformative voyage that lies ahead. May this book be your guide as you navigate the decisions and complexities of life, making choices that lead not just to temporary pleasures, but to enduring happiness and success. The content of these pages does more than merely advocate for a slower approach to life; it illuminates the pathway to a more rewarding and meaningful existence.

As the old saying goes, good things come to those who wait. As you embark on this journey, let each page inspire you to reflect on the value of waiting, to recognize the strength in restraint, and to discover the profound wisdom that lies in the power of pause.

—Roger L. Brooks

The Publisher

Dedication

I humbly dedicate this book to the unwavering pillars of my life—the incomparable Dr. Allison Ann Justo, my beloved wife, and our three extraordinary children, Emilio Jr., Joey, and Annaliese. Your presence in my journey has been the vibrant melody, the heartbeat accompanying every triumph and challenge.

To my dearest Allison, you transcend the role of mere spouse; you are my confidante, guiding star, mentor, and fierce champion of my dreams. Your unwavering love forms the bedrock of my strength, and your wisdom serves as the compass steering me through life's tumultuous seas. In your embrace, I find solace, and in your partnership, boundless inspiration. This book stands as a testament to the profound impact of your love on my soul—a love that transcends time and space.

Emilio Jr., Joey, and Annaliese—my greatest treasures—these words are dedicated to you. You are the beating heart of my legacy, the living embodiment of all that I hold dear. Each page echoes my love for you, eternally imprinted as a testament to the dreams we've shared, the laughter embraced, and the unbreakable bond we hold. As you navigate your journeys, may these words be a compass, guiding you through landscapes of dreams, resilience, and delayed gratification.

This book is not simply a collection of thoughts; it is a symphony of our shared experiences, the embodiment of the passion that burns within my soul for each of you. I am eternally grateful for the joy you bring, the lessons you teach, and the profound purpose you infuse into every moment of my existence. As I leave this legacy, know that my love for you transcends the confines of these pages and will endure until the end of time.

Contents

Introduction: What is Delayed Gratification?

> *"The ability to discipline yourself to delay gratification in the short term to enjoy greater rewards in the long term is the indispensable prerequisite for success."* — Brian Tracy

In the annals of history, countless tales are told of individuals transcending adversity, emerging triumphant through stories marked by perseverance, resilience, and an unwavering commitment to delayed gratification. At its core, delayed gratification is the art of forgoing immediate pleasures in favor of long-term goals and ambitions—a concept that underpins the very essence of success. It is a principle that I intimately understand and embrace, shaped by my own life's journey as a Cuban refugee.

My name is Emilio Justo, a Cuban immigrant who, at the tender age of three, fled the oppressive regime of Fidel Castro's communism in search of freedom and a better life. As I embark on sharing my experiences and insights in this book, it is imperative to delve into the fundamental concept of delayed gratification. This principle has guided me, shaping my perspective and enabling me to overcome seemingly insurmountable obstacles.

Delayed gratification can be likened to sowing the seeds of effort and discipline in the fertile soil of patience, nurturing them over time, and reaping the bountiful harvest resulting from steadfast dedication. It involves the willingness to forgo immediate pleasures or rewards in pursuit of loftier aspirations, making choices today that promise a better tomorrow. It forms the cornerstone of achievement in every facet of life.

In our fast-paced world, the allure of instant gratification is ubiquitous. Advertisements bombard us with promises of immediate solutions, quick fixes, and shortcuts to success. While tempting, embracing this culture of instant gratification risks sacrificing the potential for long-lasting, meaningful accomplishments.

My journey as an immigrant serves as a testament to the power of delayed gratification—a narrative of sacrifice, persistence, and an unwavering belief in the promise of a brighter future. To understand the essence of delayed gratification, let me transport you back to my early years in Cuba, a time when the island nation underwent a profound transformation under Fidel Castro's rule.

In the 1960s, Cuba experienced a revolution that promised equality but delivered oppression. Fidel Castro's communist regime sought to eradicate individual liberties, stifle dissent, and impose a rigid ideology upon its citizens. It was a period of great upheaval, as families like mine confronted the stark reality of a future marked by political persecution, economic hardship, and a pervasive sense of despair.

As a young child, I bore witness to the sacrifices my parents were willing to make for the sake of our family's future. Their profound understanding of delayed gratification would go on to shape my comprehension of this concept. They recognized that the path to success was not paved with immediate rewards but rather marked by enduring commitment and unwavering determination.

In the dead of night, we embarked on a perilous journey to escape the clutches of Castro's regime. Fidel Castro's changes to the national currency prompted my father's distrust, leading him to bury his money in the backyard. Later, he utilized this "old" currency, with far greater value than the new one, to purchase airline tickets from a Canadian diplomat, enabling us to leave Cuba via Mexico. The plane that carried us away was a vessel of hope, but also one of uncertainty, leaving behind our homeland, possessions, and loved ones in pursuit of the elusive promise of freedom.

Our journey was fraught with danger as we navigated treacherous waters in Mexico, facing the constant threat of losing what little we had. It demanded utmost patience and resilience as we endured months in Mexico with scant possessions. Finally, after patiently waiting, a Christian church in Gary, Indiana, sponsored our entry into the United States.

Reflecting on those trying times, our escape from Cuba stands as the ultimate manifestation of delayed gratification. We were willing to endure present hardships to secure a better future for ourselves and future generations—a journey that tested our resolve and necessitated sacrifices with long-term dividends.

Upon arriving in the United States, we encountered new challenges as immigrants with little more than a dream and a determination to succeed. The road ahead was arduous, and success far from guaranteed, but we embraced the principles of delayed gratification once more.

In the land of opportunity, I witnessed the transformative power of hard work and perseverance.

Delayed gratification turned aspirations into reality as my family worked tirelessly to build a new life. My father held two full-time jobs, my mother pursued education in Bloomington, Indiana, and I was sent to grow up with my grandparents in Tarkio, Missouri. Sacrifices in the short term, foregoing immediate comforts and luxuries were made to invest in our long-term goals.

Through my college and medical education, embarking on an ophthalmology career, I carried the lessons of delayed gratification with me. Understanding that success was a marathon, not a sprint, I knew the rewards of patience and persistence far surpassed the allure of instant gratification. This philosophy guided my choices and shaped my approach to life.

In the pages that follow, I will delve deeper into the concept of delayed gratification and its profound impact on the pursuit of success. Sharing personal anecdotes, insights, and strategies, I aim to illuminate the complexities of life as an immigrant and the realization of my version of the American dream.

This book is a testament to the enduring power of delayed gratification—a principle that transcends cultural, geographic, and generational boundaries. It possesses the potential to transform lives, empowering individuals to overcome adversity, realize their full potential, and achieve the success they desire.

As we embark on this shared journey, I invite you to reflect on your life and contemplate the role of delayed gratification in your pursuit of success. What sacrifices are you willing to make today for a brighter tomorrow? What dreams and aspirations do you hold dear, and how can the principles of delayed gratification guide you towards their realization?

In the chapters ahead, we will explore the various facets of delayed gratification, ranging from setting and pursuing long-term goals to cultivating discipline and resilience. The exploration will delve into the psychology behind delayed gratification, showcasing its potential as a powerful tool for personal and professional growth.

Drawing from my experiences as a Cuban refugee, I aim to inspire and empower you to embrace the principles of delayed gratification and embark on your journey toward success. Together, we will uncover that delayed gratification is not merely a concept; it is a way of life, a philosophy capable of leading to profound transformation and fulfillment.

My journey is not unique; it echoes the countless stories of immigrants and dreamers worldwide who have embraced delayed gratification to conquer challenges and achieve aspirations. Let us join forces in uncovering the power of deferred rewards and celebrating the triumph of the human spirit in the face of adversity.

Now, as we begin this voyage of self-discovery and personal growth, we will explore the art of delayed gratification and reveal the secrets to achieving success—lessons learned through the eyes of an immigrant who dared to dream and persist. This book unveils the transformative power of patience, perseverance, and the resilience of the human spirit, examined through the lens of an immigrant's odyssey.

Chapter 1

The Nature of Delayed Gratification

"The more you can contain your desires and impulses, the more you will be able to enjoy greater freedom, success, and peace of mind." – Brian Tracy

"Instant gratification takes too long." – *Carrie Fisher*

The concept of delayed gratification emerges not merely as a product of modern psychology or a strategy for success. Instead, it is deeply woven into the very fabric of our DNA, a legacy passed down through the millennia by our ancestors. These early humans, as cave-dwelling hunters and gatherers, pioneered the path to survival by mastering the art of patience.

In the primal embrace of nature, the fundamental concept of delayed gratification found its roots, intricately etched in the essence of survival. Our ancestors, the cave dwellers, navigated the untamed terrains of a world untouched by modern convenience. In this raw and challenging environment, they became intimately familiar with the art of waiting. The hunt, a primal pursuit for sustenance, epitomized this patience—an understanding that rewards required effort, time, and strategic planning.

The Ancestral Roots of Delayed Gratification

Imagine, for a moment, the life of our distant ancestors—the prehistoric humans who roamed the Earth long before the advent of convenience stores, smartphones, or instant delivery services. In this era, these early Homo sapiens faced a world where the next meal was never guaranteed, and survival hinged on their ability to adapt to the rhythms of nature, exercising patience in the pursuit of sustenance.

In this primeval existence, gratification was inevitably delayed. The hunt for nourishment transcended mere convenience; it was a life-or-death endeavor. Our ancestors had to attune themselves to the environment, tracking the movements of prey, understanding the changing seasons, and patiently awaiting the opportune moment to strike. They comprehended that impulsive actions could lead to starvation, so they honed their ability to delay immediate desires in favor of long-term survival.

Delayed gratification was not just a choice; it was a necessity ingrained in the fabric of their daily lives. The patience required for the hunt, the cultivation of crops, and the construction of shelters stood as testaments to the power of delayed gratification in ensuring the continuation of the human species. Through waiting, planning, and strategizing for future rewards, our ancestors forged a path that allowed humanity to endure and thrive.

Nature, in its wisdom, whispered to our forebears that rewards held a sweeter essence when earned through patience and persistence. The gratification derived from a successful hunt was not instantaneous; it was the culmination of days, sometimes weeks, filled with the intricate dance of tracking, waiting, and striving for the opportune moment. The energy expended in this primal pursuit, coupled with strategic planning and the anticipation of a delayed reward, composed a captivating dance—a primal lesson echoing the intrinsic value of patience.

The Modern Dilemma: Instant Gratification vs. Delayed Gratification

"Don't let the fear of the time it will take to accomplish something stand in the way of your doing it. The time will pass anyway; we might just as well put that passing time to the best possible use."
– Earl Nightingale

Fast forward to the present day, and the world has undergone a dizzying transformation. We have progressed from being hunters and gatherers to becoming creators and consumers, surrounded by an abundance of choices and instant pleasures. While the conveniences of modern life undeniably enhance our quality of life in numerous ways, they concurrently give rise to a paradox—a tension between the ancient wisdom of delayed gratification and the allure of immediate rewards.

In the modern world, marked by technological advances and societal progress, the dynamics of gratification have experienced a profound shift. The accessibility to instant rewards, propelled by technological advancements, has instigated a paradigm shift in how we perceive and pursue gratification. The ascent of the "instant gratification culture" has become emblematic of our times. A growing number of teenagers and young adults find themselves captivated by the notion that fame, fortune, and material wealth can be effortlessly attained through social media platforms such as Instagram, Facebook, TikTok, and the like. Many youths entertain the belief that they can circumvent the demands of hard work, perseverance, and determination with the mere "click of a button." A notable trend emerges where some young individuals express the sentiment that college is unnecessary for their success, citing its seemingly protracted duration as a deterrent. The decline in college enrollment since 2010 is, in part, a reflection of today's youth yearning for instant success. This shifting mindset poses challenges and prompts a critical examination of the values and expectations prevalent in contemporary society.

In an era of smartphones, fast food, and one-click shopping, our lives have become accustomed to immediacy. Our desires can be effortlessly satisfied with the touch of a screen or the press of a button. We enjoy access to an abundance of information, entertainment, and products, all readily available with minimal effort. However, amid this age of instant gratification, have we unwittingly sacrificed something essential to our well-being? I would firmly argue that the answer is "yes."

The Price of Privilege

"The privilege of a lifetime is being who
you are."
– Joseph Campbell

The conveniences and privileges bestowed by modern life, undoubtedly remarkable as they may be, come with a cost—a cost often overlooked that strikes at the heart of our discussion. The price of privilege, in the context of instant gratification, is intricate and far-reaching.

However, as we immerse ourselves in this age of convenience, we must also confront the repercussions of instant gratification. The cost of privilege often manifests as the erosion of paticnce—a decline in our ability to delay gratification. In our relentless pursuit of efficiency and ease, we may find ourselves disconnected from the profound satisfaction derived from waiting and diligently working towards a goal.

To illustrate, my two teenage sons assert that the educational journey to become a physician takes too long, expressing a preference to attend college, obtain a degree, and promptly enter the workforce. Despite my repeated attempts to explain that the seemingly extended educational process (four years of college, four years of medical school, and over four years of residency) might initially appear lengthy, the outcome is one of immense satisfaction. Upon commencing medical practice, they would be rewarded financially right away, in contrast to working their way through a series of jobs after college, where the financial returns would likely be only a fraction of what they could achieve as physicians.

Certainly, the goal should never be solely focused on money or financial success. However, in the minds of many teenagers, this aspect often takes precedence. Hence, I provide a tangible example from my own family to underscore this point. Teenagers often feel that having to wait until the age of 26-30 to earn "significant money" is an overly protracted process. Furthermore, the prospect of hard work and dedicated perseverance required to navigate the extensive educational journey, coupled with the multitude of examinations, tends to induce stress even before the process begins.

On the flip side, instant gratification tends to offer immediate pleasure but frequently at the expense of long-term fulfillment. It may foster impulsiveness, a lack of resilience, and a diminished ability to withstand challenges. The insatiable desire for instant rewards has the potential to impede the development of crucial life skills, including perseverance, discipline, and delayed gratification—skills that are indispensable for achieving meaningful success in various aspects of life. The concept of privilege operates as a double-edged sword within instant gratification. On one hand, privilege can afford individuals access to resources and opportunities that may pave the way for a more comfortable and convenient life.

On the other hand, this privilege can inadvertently cultivate a desire for immediate rewards and instant satisfaction. This phenomenon is particularly pronounced among today's youth, who are coming of age in a world defined by technological advances and a culture that caters to instant gratification.

Privilege, whether stemming from socioeconomic status, access to quality education, or a supportive family environment, can create a paradox for young individuals. On one side of the paradox, privilege provides a cushion of comfort, reducing the necessity to confront immediate hardships. Yet, this comfort can instigate a craving for quick, easy solutions, often manifesting as a thirst for instant gratification.

For instance, the fact that my children were born into privilege, with all the material, educational, and financial comforts provided to them, is a contributing factor to their seeming lack of urgency to delay gratification and persevere through the hardships of education for a long-term goal. Instead, they aspire to achieve the same or even greater levels of success than their father but in a fraction of the time invested. Influenced by the surrounding buzz from friends, social media, television, and the entertainment industry, my sons are convinced that they can attain loftier goals in shorter durations—beliefs nurtured by their privilege. In this context, recognizing and embracing one's authentic self is a valuable privilege in life. It signifies that authenticity, in and of itself, holds greater value than the pursuit of instant or superficial forms of gratification.

Instant Gratification Results in Increased Negative Traits

Loss of Patience: In a world where everything is at our fingertips, patience has become a scarce commodity. The expectation for immediate results, quick fixes, and instant gratification permeates all aspects of life. This impatience poses a threat to our ability to pursue long-term goals, cultivate meaningful relationships, and endure discomfort on the journey to success.

Short-Term Thinking: The culture of instant gratification often cultivates a short-term mindset. When our desires are consistently met in the present moment, there's a risk of losing focus on the future. This short-term thinking can impede our ability to plan, save, and invest in our long-term well-being.

For instance, I succumbed to this mindset during the 2005-2007 period when residential real estate was booming. It was remarkably easy to acquire rental properties with little or no money down. Driven by my desire for instant gratification, I purchased over twenty rental homes in less than a year with minimal upfront investment. Unfortunately, this coincided with the peak of the real estate market when property values were at an all-time high. With the minimal down payment, my monthly mortgage payments far exceeded the rental income received from tenants. This experience served as a significant lesson in forsaking my principles, particularly my commitment to delayed gratification.

Ultimately, to avert bankruptcy, I had to release these properties one by one. It was a stark realization that I had succumbed to the allure of a "get rich quick" scenario, a departure from my core beliefs in perseverance, due diligence, and self-discipline.

"The best time to plant a tree was twenty years ago. The second-best time is now."
– Chinese Proverb

Emotional Toll: Paradoxically, the pursuit of instant gratification can leave individuals feeling unsatisfied and unfulfilled. The dopamine rush of immediate pleasure can be fleeting, leading to a cycle of seeking more and more to fill the void, which can take a toll on mental and emotional health.

In my professional career working with patients in cosmetic/aesthetic medicine, I have observed a pattern. Patients often seek quick fixes, such as cosmetic surgery or non-surgical treatments, to experience instant gratification and a boost in self-esteem. However, these feelings tend to fade quickly, leading to a cycle of addiction. Patients return for additional procedures, seeking instant gratification repeatedly in an attempt to find their fountain of youth. Instead of embracing aging gracefully, this pursuit becomes a never-ending race without a finish line. I've encountered situations where I had to decline procedures, either because the patient already looked great and chasing perfection was risky, or because excessive prior cosmetic work had resulted in an unnatural appearance. This can be counter-intuitive to the reader's expectations.

"Often, it's not about becoming a new
person, but becoming the person you were
meant to be, and already are, but don't know
how to be."
– Heath L. Buckmaster

Financial Implications: The culture of instant gratification can have significant financial consequences, leading to overspending, debt, and a lack of financial preparedness for the future.

Reflecting on my own experience, I recognized the importance of long-term care insurance when I was approximately thirty-five years old. Influenced by a mentor physician and an insurance agent, I invested in a comprehensive policy for my mother, considering the responsibility I would bear as her only child, especially in her later years.

Over the years, I paid what seemed like substantial insurance premiums, only to be both shocked and relieved when, after fifteen years of payments, my mother's health significantly declined. She needed assisted living and, later, skilled nursing/memory care due to advanced dementia. Remarkably, the long-term care insurance I had invested in for years proved invaluable, covering her monthly expenses in full. Not only did she receive care in top-quality facilities, but the insurance payout far exceeded the premiums I had paid. This experience underscored the wisdom and prudence of investing in long-term care insurance as a forward-looking financial strategy.

"The safe way to double your money is to fold it over once and put it in your pocket."
– Kin Hubbard

Diminished Resilience: Delayed gratification serves as a crucible for building resilience, imparting the ability to endure discomfort, setbacks, and challenges in the pursuit of long-term goals. In contrast, succumbing to instant gratification can potentially render individuals more fragile in the face of adversity.

An illustrative example from my personal experience involves my twelve-year-old daughter during her seventh-grade academic year. She encountered significant anxiety in her mathematics class due to the strict and challenging teaching methodology of her new teacher. As concerned parents, my wife and I initially felt the urge to intervene, meet with the teacher, and swiftly resolve the issues on behalf of our daughter.

However, after thoughtful consideration, we opted for a different approach. Instead of directly intervening, we encouraged our daughter to take the initiative. We advised her to compile itemized notes outlining her concerns and anxieties, and then independently meet with the math department chairperson. Subsequently, she would engage in a direct conversation with her new math teacher to discuss each issue herself, without our immediate involvement.

Resisting the temptation to swiftly resolve the situation for her, we aimed to teach our daughter valuable lessons in building strength and resilience. This approach allowed her to confront challenges independently, develop problem-solving skills, enhance her communication abilities, and ultimately build resilience.

The intention was to empower her to handle similar issues autonomously in the future, fostering a sense of self-reliance and fortitude.

"The greatest glory in living lies not in never falling, but in rising every time we fall."
– Nelson Mandela

Striking a Balance: Embracing Nature's Wisdom in the Modern World

"While our civilization has expanded our opportunities, it has not improved our spirit and sense of moral values."
– Herbert Hoover

In this chapter, we explore the contrast between our primal instincts for patience and the contemporary allure of instant gratification. We reflect on how understanding and embracing the lessons of nature can guide us to find a balance—a balance that enables us to enjoy the benefits of modern progress while still appreciating the value of patience and delayed gratification.

Nature reminds us that waiting, strategizing, and putting in the effort can yield rewards beyond our immediate desires. As we navigate this modern landscape of quick fixes and convenience, let us heed these ancient whispers and rekindle the virtue of patience, for it is through patience that we shall find lasting and meaningful fulfillment.

Our journey unfolds as we explore the roots of delayed gratification in the context of our ancestral past and grapple with the challenges posed by the contemporary culture of instant gratification. Throughout the upcoming chapters, we will uncover strategies and insights that can help us harness the wisdom of patience, strike a balance with the allure of instant rewards, and unlock the transformative power of delayed gratification on our path to success and fulfillment.

Chapter 2

The Power of Clearly Defined Long-Term Goals

In the intricate tapestry of success, the foundational weave is formed by defining and pursuing long-term goals. Just as a skilled architect envisions a grand structure before placing the first brick, a successful individual must clearly articulate their long-term goals. This vision acts as a compass, guiding actions, and a lighthouse, illuminating the path through the fog of uncertainty. In this chapter, we will delve into the profound importance of clearly defining your most significant long-term goals, expressing them in writing, and allowing them to serve as a perpetual reminder of your aspirations. The clarity provided by well-defined long-term goals has the potential to guide your actions, choices, and daily life toward the realization of your dreams.

The Significance of Clear Long-Term Goals

Long-term goals act as the lighthouses guiding the ships of our lives through the unpredictable seas of existence. They offer direction, purpose, and a roadmap for achieving what truly matters. Here's why they hold such significance:

Guidance and Focus in Decision-Making: Clarity in long-term goals serves as a compass for decision-making. When confronted with choices or opportunities, a clear vision of your long-term objectives helps assess whether a particular option aligns with your desired destination. It acts as a safeguard against drifting off course, keeping your focus on actions that propel you closer to your aspirations. Well-defined long-term goals also assist in precisely outlining what you aim to achieve, preventing you from getting lost in the maze of distractions and immediate desires. With a defined goal, you can efficiently allocate your time and resources to the most meaningful pursuits.

A compelling example from my own life is following my TEDx talk on August 12, 2023, at TEDxCherry-CreekHS on "Delayed Gratification: Your Superpower to Success." Subsequently, I made a deliberate decision to channel my time and energy into writing a book that imparts the principles of delayed gratification that have profoundly influenced my life and led to significant opportunities and success. This ambition ranks among my most meaningful pursuits, and despite maintaining a full-time medical practice, I have maintained a laser-like focus in bringing this goal to fruition. It exemplifies the type of focus and mindset I advocate for each person— setting a compass for a direct path forward to continually strive toward their destination.

Motivation and Persistence: Goals provide you with a reason to wake up every morning with enthusiasm. Consider the example of writing this book. Despite dedicating fifty hours per week to my traditional career, the goal of completing this book and sharing my message with the world keeps me focused, motivated, and eager for more! Goals infuse your actions with purpose, creating a driving force that propels you forward. The prospect of achieving a long-term goal can serve as a powerful motivator, especially when the path is challenging. Well-defined long-term goals inject motivation into your daily endeavors. When faced with challenges, envisioning the ultimate reward awaiting you at the end of the journey can reignite your determination. The mental image of achievement fuels persistence and helps you navigate storms on your path to success.

Measure of Progress: Long-term goals provide a specific means to measure your progress, allowing you to gauge how much closer you are to your aspirations. This tracking of progress can boost confidence and instill a sense of accomplishment. Long-term goals also serve as benchmarks against which you can measure your achievements, acting as yardsticks to evaluate both the distance covered and the distance yet to be traversed. Celebrating milestones, whether large or small, brings a sense of accomplishment, reinforcing your belief in your ability to reach your ultimate objectives.

Crucially, it's important to celebrate each small milestone achieved, recognizing that a series of small victories leads to the attainment of greater milestones. Celebrating, however, should be approached with caution, as the term may have different meanings for each reader. In my opinion, it is imperative not to get side-tracked in the pursuit of ultimate objectives by celebrating too extrinsically, such as going to dinner or having a drink. Instead, I advocate for celebrating more intrinsically—reflecting on the moment and the small victory, complimenting oneself on the achievement, and using this knowledge as a tool and resource to gain the next victory more efficiently. Regardless of the chosen method to celebrate milestones, it is essential to stay focused and on track, ensuring that the celebration itself does not become a distraction from the ultimate goal.

Alignment and Focus: Defining long-term goals ensures that your actions and efforts are aligned with a central purpose, filtering out distractions and endeavors that might steer you off track. This alignment enables laser-like focus on activities that propel you toward your envisioned future.

For instance, during my college and medical school years, my focus was squarely on completing the necessary studies over the years to ultimately achieve my goal of becoming an eye surgeon and running my medical practice. Throughout this journey, I had to avoid being distracted by the seemingly long and arduous path. Instead, I learned to enjoy the process, immersing myself with dedicated focus. Nearing the end of my studies, I found such fulfillment in the journey that I briefly entertained the idea of attending law school after completing medical school. This illustrates the power of maintaining focus and alignment with long-term goals, even when faced with tempting diversions along the way.

Enhanced Time Management: Knowing your long-term goals plays a crucial role in effective time management. It allows you to prioritize tasks and allocate time based on their relevance to your objectives. This focused approach optimizes the use of your time and resources, ultimately leading to greater efficiency and productivity, adhering to the adage of "work smarter, not harder." Time management is a critical aspect of success in all areas of life.

In general, I find that time management tends to be lacking in many youths, especially teenagers. It becomes all too easy to slip into the mindset of doing the minimum to get by in the moment, while spending valuable time on activities like social media, watching TV, hanging out with friends, or going to the gym. While I advocate for a balanced life with good physical and emotional health, as well as sociability, it's crucial to emphasize the importance of being a master of time. This mastery is necessary to accomplish the more important long-term goals promptly rather than succumbing to procrastination.

Resilience: When life presents challenges and setbacks, long-term goals serve as a source of resilience. They remind you why you embarked on this journey in the first place, enabling you to weather the storms and persist in the face of adversity. Resilience, for some, is a natural trait, while others must consciously cultivate this skill.

Reflecting on my journey as a Cuban refugee coming to the United States, resilience played a pivotal role in shaping my character. Faced with numerous obstacles such as learning the English language and lacking the comfort of privilege, I relied on resilience to overcome adversity. Love and nurturing within the family and from dear friends played a crucial role in cultivating this resilience.

An example of resilience in my life is evident in our middle child, who has confronted significant challenges such as severe acne, anaphylactic allergies to all nuts, and a rare medical syndrome affecting his ability to walk comfortably and have steady hands. Despite these challenges, he has demonstrated tremendous self-discipline in school, achieving academic success while simultaneously balancing his commitment to becoming a bodybuilder in the gym. This example underscores the power of resilience in overcoming adversity and pursuing long-term goals despite formidable obstacles.

Recommendations for Defining Long-Term Goals

To harness the power of long-term goals, you must clearly define them. The following recommendations will guide you in this process:

1. Reflect on Your Values and Passions

Begin by introspecting and identifying what truly matters to you. Consider your passions, values, and principles that resonate with your authentic self. Ask yourself: What truly matters to you? In which areas of life do you find the most joy and fulfillment? Aligning your long-term goals with your core beliefs ensures a meaningful and fulfilling journey consistent with the fundamental aspects of your identity.

— 66 —

"Your time is limited, don't waste
it living someone else's life."
– Steve Jobs

— 99 —

2. Create an Action Plan

An action plan serves as your roadmap for achieving your long-term goals. It outlines the necessary steps, required resources, and timeline for each milestone, breaking down the seemingly insurmountable journey into manageable tasks. Your action plan should be realistic yet push you to stretch beyond your comfort zone.

In the words of author Grant Cardone, it's advisable to create an action plan and set goals that are much higher than your initial desires. In retrospect, you may find that the goals and action plan initially set are more easily achievable than originally imagined. Therefore, it's essential to push yourself to stretch beyond your traditional thinking to achieve greatness.

> "Without goals, and plans to reach them, you are like a ship that has set sail with no destination."
> – Fitzhugh Dodson

3. Be Specific and Measurable

Use the SMART (Specific, Measurable, Achievable, Relevant, Time-bound) criteria to structure your long-term goals. Be precise about what you want to achieve, ensuring that you can measure progress, setting attainable targets that are relevant to your vision, and establishing a clear timeline for accomplishment.

Your long-term goals must be specific and measurable. Rather than stating a vague ambition like "I want to be successful," define what success means to you. For instance, your goal could be "I want to become a respected published author with at least five bestselling books." This level of specificity enables you to track your progress and know when you've achieved your goal.

> "A goal properly set is halfway reached."
> – Zig Ziglar

4. Prioritize and Categorize

Categorize your long-term goals based on different aspects of your life, such as career, relationships, personal growth, health, and finances. Prioritize them to identify the most critical objectives that will have the most significant impact on your life. By categorizing your goals, you can work on achieving each of them simultaneously, recognizing that they will inexplicably and exponentially compound with each other. This strategic approach allows for holistic development across various facets of your life.

> "You can do anything, but not everything."
> – David Allen

5. Break Down Goals into Milestones

Long-term goals can feel overwhelming if they're too broad. To make them more manageable, break them down into smaller milestones. Each milestone should represent a significant step toward the ultimate goal, serving as a stepping stone in your journey. By breaking down the larger objective into achievable steps, you'll experience a sense of progress and remain motivated to keep advancing. Achieving these milestones not only signifies progress but also helps build momentum, maintaining your motivation throughout the journey toward your long-term objectives.

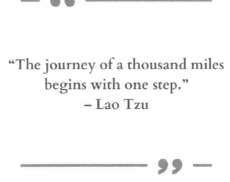

"The journey of a thousand miles begins with one step."
– Lao Tzu

6. Set Realistic Timeframes

Establish realistic timeframes for your long-term goals by considering the amount of time and effort required to achieve them. Be cautious not to set unrealistically short deadlines that may lead to frustration. Simultaneously, avoid making your timelines too distant, as this can diminish a sense of urgency. Ensure that you write down your timeframes and regularly chart your progress. This approach allows you to celebrate milestones along the way, providing both a sense of accomplishment and the opportunity to reassess and adjust your plan if needed.

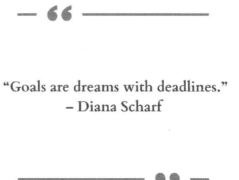

"Goals are dreams with deadlines."
– Diana Scharf

7. Write Down Your Goals

The act of writing your long-term goals down is pivotal. It transforms an abstract idea into a tangible commitment. When you put your goals on paper, you create a contract with yourself, making it more likely that you will take them seriously. Whenever possible, dedicate 5-10 minutes daily to re-write your goals, and if necessary, modify them. Repeat them both out loud and to yourself to create a positive affirmation for yourself daily. This regular practice not only reinforces your commitment but also helps keep your long-term goals at the forefront of your consciousness, enhancing focus and determination.

"The act of writing down a goal makes it real."
– Les Brown

8. Make Your Goals Visible

Bring your goals to life by creating a vision board. Utilize images, quotes, and visuals that represent your objectives and aspirations. Place the vision board in a visible spot where you'll encounter it daily. This visual reminder serves to reinforce your goals, keeping them at the forefront of your mind. Regular exposure to your vision board enhances motivation and provides a tangible representation of the future you are striving to achieve.

"Big things have small beginnings."
– T.E. Lawrence (Lawrence of Arabia)

9. Regularly Review and Revise

Set aside regular times to review your long-term goals. During these sessions, assess your progress, celebrate achievements—whether large or small—and adapt your strategy if needed. As you progress toward your long-term goals, periodically review and, if necessary, revise them. It's possible that your aspirations evolve or that your priorities shift. Regularly assessing your goals ensures that they remain relevant and aligned with your ever-changing life. Keep in mind that life is dynamic, and circumstances change. It's essential to ensure your goals remain relevant and be willing to adjust them as needed.

"If you're not making mistakes,
then you're not doing anything."
– John Wooden

10. Write a Personal Mission Statement

Craft a mission statement that encapsulates your overarching purpose and objectives. This succinct declaration serves as a guiding principle, encapsulating your values and long-term goals. It reinforces your vision and serves as a touchstone for decision-making. It is okay if your mission statement changes along the way, as this journey is ever-evolving, and it is imperative to stay true to oneself. Regularly revisiting and updating your mission statement ensures that it remains a true reflection of your values and aspirations throughout your evolving journey.

— 66 —

"The purpose of life is not to be happy. It is to be useful, to be honorable, to be compassionate, to have it make some difference that you have lived and lived well."
– Ralph Waldo Emerson

99 —

11. Seek Accountability and Support

Share your long-term goals with a trusted friend, mentor, or coach who can provide guidance and hold you accountable. Accountability fosters responsibility, motivating you to stay on track and take ownership of your journey. If possible, seek out someone whom you trust and respect, and who has achieved greater things than you have. Use this person's experience as a gauge to assist you in your success. Regular check-ins with your chosen confidant provide an external perspective, valuable insights, and encouragement, enhancing your ability to navigate challenges and achieve your long-term goals.

"Surround yourself with only people
who are going to lift you higher."
– Oprah

12. Share Your Goals Selectively

While it's essential to share your goals with a few trusted individuals who can offer support and accountability, exercise caution when sharing your ambitions widely; unnecessary exposure may invite unsolicited opinions or negative energy, which could deter you from your path. In a karmic environment, it's possible that some individuals around you, including friends, family, or trusted advisors, may be subconsciously envious of your internal drive, your goals, and even your success.

Keep in mind that, at times, it may be family members who unintentionally shed negative energy on your desires, questioning why you work so hard or suggesting you should relax more. This unintentional negativity can detract from your long-term objectives, motivations, and ultimately your success. Be discerning about whom you share your goals with and choose individuals who genuinely support and uplift your aspirations.

"Don't tell people your dreams. Show them."
– Unknown

13. Stay Committed and Persistent

Commit to your long-term goals with unwavering determination. Embrace the positive connotation of "obsession" to foster determination, perseverance, commitment, and self-discipline. Maintain persistence even in the face of challenges and setbacks. Treat setbacks as valuable learning experiences, allowing them to refine your approach and strengthen your resolve. Understand that failures are an inherent part of the journey towards success. Embrace failures, always learn from them, and then stay committed, focused, and driven to continue pursuing your long-term objectives. This resilience and commitment are key to overcoming obstacles and achieving lasting success.

> "Our greatest weakness lies in giving up. The most certain way to succeed is always to try just one more time."
> – Thomas A. Edison

14. Stay Flexible

While the importance of setting clear long-term goals cannot be overstated, it's equally important to remain flexible. Life is unpredictable, and circumstances can change. Your goals should adapt to these changes rather than become rigid obstacles.

For instance, in my life, after giving my first TEDx talk in August 2023 outside of Denver, Colorado at TEDxCherryCreekHS, the well-received talk with millions of YouTube views led me to decide to write this book. However, while writing this book, I applied to speak at a different TEDx event on the obsession advantage for unparalleled success, which was accepted. So, by the time you are reading this book, I will have presented my second TEDx talk in London, Ontario, Canada in February 2024 at TEDxWesternU. Along this journey, another opportunity emerged to speak in India amongst several hundreds of thousands of their native people, highlighting the necessity of flexibility as the journey keeps evolving. This constant evaluation and re-evaluation of goals are integral, and the excitement lies in participating and evolving within the journey, acknowledging that reaching a final destination might be a dynamic and ever-changing concept.

"Stay committed to your decisions but
stay flexible in your approach."
– Tony Robbins

15. Visualize Success

Spend time visualizing the successful realization of your long-term goals. Immerse yourself in the emotions and experiences associated with achieving your objectives. Allow your mind to paint a detailed picture of your success, engaging all your senses in this mental imagery. This vivid visualization reinforces your commitment and primes your subconscious mind to actively work toward your goals. By regularly immersing yourself in these positive mental images, you enhance your focus, motivation, and belief in your ability to achieve the long-term success you aspire to.

—— 66 ——

"The only limit to our realization of
tomorrow will be our doubts of today."
– Franklin D. Roosevelt

—— 99 ——

Conclusion: The Beacon of Your Dreams

Clearly defined long-term goals act as guiding beacons, illuminating the path toward your aspirations. Articulating and keeping these goals visible is comparable to charting a course through unexplored waters. The clarity obtained and the guidance offered in your journey toward success are immeasurable. These goals provide essential direction, motivation, and a sense of purpose, acting as a steadfast companion through life's challenges. By adhering to these recommendations and heeding the wisdom of precisely defined objectives, individuals empower themselves to navigate life's complexities with purpose, determination, and unwavering focus. The commitment to the journey of goal setting enables individuals to transform aspirations into reality.

Chapter 3

The Foundations of Success - Prioritizing Education and Self-Improvement

In the grand symphony of life, the harmonies of success often originate from the pursuit of knowledge and self-improvement. This chapter explores the profound significance of prioritizing education and self-improvement, transcending the limitations of age, experience, and wisdom. The exploration navigates through principles highlighting the importance of investing in oneself mentally, emotionally, spiritually, and financially, embracing the continuous process of learning and skill acquisition. The narrative unravels the indispensable role that dedication to physical and spiritual health plays in this endeavor, akin to the perpetual flame of curiosity that guides us, reminiscent of a young child's unrelenting quest for understanding. Additionally, the discussion explores the principles emphasizing that investing in oneself is the most invaluable and enduring investment one can make.

"The best investment you can make is
in yourself."
– Warren Buffett

Warren Buffett's words encapsulate the core message of this section, highlighting the paramount importance of self-investment. It emphasizes that the unwavering dedication to lifelong learning and self-improvement constitutes the foundation of enduring success. In a world teeming with boundless opportunities and information readily accessible at our fingertips, there exists both a privilege and a responsibility to invest in one's education and personal growth. The pursuit of knowledge, the honing of skills, and the steadfast commitment to self-improvement stand as the pillars that propel us to new heights.

The Importance of Investing in Yourself, Education, and Self-Improvement

The path toward delayed gratification begins with a steadfast commitment to self-investment. It is a journey that yields dividends not in currency but in the currency of knowledge, growth, and personal fulfillment. Education serves as the vessel propelling us forward, casting us not as passive travelers but as active explorers.

"Education is the kindling of a flame, not
the filling of a vessel."
– Socrates

Socrates' insight poignantly conveys that education is not merely about passive accumulation but, more importantly, the ignition of curiosity and the cultivation of personal growth.

An illustrative example comes from my wife's experience. Independently, she embarked on months of online research to master the intricacies of forensic genetic genealogy, transforming herself into a proficient "DNA detective." Her dedication was so profound that she successfully located specific living, previously missing family members within her ancestral tree.

Education, as exemplified by Socrates and echoed in my wife's journey, transcends the notion of stuffing facts and figures into an empty container. Instead, it is the dynamic process of kindling a curiosity-driven flame within. This flame, once ignited, brightly illuminates our path through the dark alleys of ignorance, guiding us toward continuous growth and self-improvement.

"The mind is not a vessel to be filled, but
a fire to be kindled."
– Plutarch

This quote serves as a poignant reminder that education and self-improvement transcend the mere accumulation of facts; instead, they are about igniting the fire of curiosity and the relentless pursuit of knowledge.

Learning is not confined to the walls of a classroom or the pages of a textbook. Rather, it unfolds as a lifelong journey, where each day offers an opportunity to broaden one's horizons. In the pursuit of delayed gratification, it becomes evident that the process of learning is akin to a marathon, not a sprint. It is a perpetual, evolving journey that knows no boundaries of age, experience, or wisdom.

"An investment in knowledge always pays
the best interest."
– Benjamin Franklin

This quotation emphasizes that regardless of age, experience, or wisdom, the most crucial investment in life is the commitment to self-improvement.

The investment in knowledge and personal growth is exemplified by a straightforward yet compelling example from my own experience. At the tender age of 9, my daughter independently expressed a desire to take babysitting and infant CPR classes. Her initiative stemmed not from any parental suggestion but from her innate craving for knowledge and responsibility. This self-driven pursuit illustrates the transformative power of investing in oneself, even at a young age, and highlights the intrinsic motivation that can ignite a flame within.

Investing Mentally, Emotionally, Spiritually, and Financially in Oneself

The investment in oneself extends beyond financial considerations, enveloping the mental, emotional, and spiritual facets of our being. The most profound and enduring wealth resides within, and this wealth is cultivated through dedicated self-investment.

"Change is the result of all true learning."
– Leo Buscaglia

Leo Buscaglia's quote reminds us that learning leads to change, evolution, and growth.

Our mental faculties stand as our most valuable assets. The capacity to think critically, solve problems, and adapt to changing circumstances is truly priceless. A commitment to self-improvement at the mental level entails the acquisition of knowledge, the honing of skills, and the fostering of a growth mindset. It signifies the acknowledgment that our minds are not stagnant reservoirs but fertile grounds capable of continuously yielding the fruits of understanding.

— 66 ——

"Learning never exhausts the mind."
– Leonardo da Vinci

—— 99 —

Leonardo da Vinci's words resonate with the timeless idea that the pursuit of knowledge serves as an inexhaustible source of inspiration.

An illustrative example of embodying this growth mindset is a habit that, unfortunately, took me many years to cultivate. During my daily 90-minute commute to and from work, I transitioned from merely listening to music, a practice I adhered to for numerous years, to immersing myself in audiobooks. This change allowed me to explore a diverse range of topics that piqued my interest, contributing to the continual growth of my mind and knowledge base. After persistently pointing out the benefits to my wife over several months, she, too, has become enamored with audiobooks. Reflecting on this transformation, I realize that had I adopted this behavior and cultivated this habit years ago, I would now be a walking encyclopedia of knowledge.

In the realm of self-investment, emotional intelligence is equally vital. Emotional resilience, empathy, and self-awareness stand as crucial components of personal growth. Mastering one's emotions not only fosters greater self-control but also cultivates healthier relationships and a more profound sense of contentment.

"Emotional intelligence is the real secret to success."
– Gary Vaynerchuk

This quote by Gary Vaynerchuk underscores the pivotal role of emotional intelligence in attaining success and personal growth. It accentuates the significance of comprehending and effectively managing one's emotions as a catalyst for positive outcomes across various facets of life.

Spiritual investment, on the other hand, is a pursuit aimed at delving into the profound questions of existence and purpose. It encompasses the cultivation of values, the quest for meaning, and the exploration of a sense of connectedness to the universe. A life enriched with spiritual depth often begets greater clarity, inner peace, and the ability to navigate life's tumultuous waters with grace.

"The soul always knows what to do to heal itself. The challenge is to silence the mind."
– Caroline Myss

This quote by Caroline Myss beautifully encapsulates the notion that nurturing our spiritual well-being and exploring profound existential questions can lead to inner healing, clarity, and peace. It suggests that the soul possesses a wisdom capable of guiding us toward a more harmonious and graceful life.

As part of our family's spiritual investment, we dedicate one day per month to volunteering at our local food bank. During this time, the children and I contribute five hours to activities such as stocking shelves, packaging food items for guests, and delivering bags of food to their vehicles. While we may feel physically tired at the end of the day, the experience rejuvenates us spiritually and emotionally. The ability to assist others and contribute to society in this small yet meaningful way becomes a source of profound fulfillment.

Financial investment in oneself represents another facet of self-improvement. This includes judicious financial planning, strategic investments in education and skill development, and the alignment of resources with long-term goals. Financial health stands as a crucial pillar of personal success, providing the necessary stability to pursue dreams and aspirations.

"Formal education will make you a living;
self-education will make you a fortune."
– Jim Rohn

Jim Rohn's insightful words underscore the difference between conventional education and the boundless potential of self-education. Self-education spans mental, emotional, spiritual, and financial growth.

Embracing the Process of Learning and Acquiring New Skills

Learning and acquiring new skills serve as the driving forces behind progress and long-term success. The educational journey doesn't conclude after formal schooling; it persists throughout life. Whether through self-directed learning, courses, mentorship, or hands-on experience, each newly acquired skill becomes a stepping stone to self-improvement.

True learning transcends the mere accumulation of facts; it involves the practical application of knowledge. It's the capacity to adapt, solve problems, and innovate. Learning not only opens doors but also sparks creativity, keeping the mind agile. It serves as the fuel propelling progress, unrestricted by age or experience.

Every new skill learned and every piece of knowledge gained contributes to personal growth, be it acquiring a new language, mastering a musical instrument, or refining a professional skill. The enrichment derived from these skills renders us more capable, confident, and versatile individuals. Moreover, learning diverse skills expands the mind, enhancing its ability to synthesize new information unrelated to the original learning. This expansion fosters an increased aptitude for learning, and information assimilation, and boosts creativity and thought processes.

Embracing the learning process necessitates a mindset that welcomes challenges and failures as opportunities for growth. This resilient approach recognizes setbacks not as roadblocks but as stepping stones on the path to mastery.

Dr. Seuss's words serve as an inspirational reminder that education and self-improvement not only expand one's knowledge, but also open doors to new opportunities and experiences.

Devotion to Physical and Spiritual Health

Physical and spiritual health are integral components of self-improvement and the pursuit of delayed gratification. The body serves as the vessel through which we experience life, and nurturing it is a fundamental aspect of personal growth.

Jim Rohn's words succinctly emphasize that your body is the vessel through which you navigate life. Taking care of it is a fundamental responsibility that enables you to pursue and achieve your aspirations.

To maximize your potential, it is essential to dedicate attention to both physical and spiritual health. These elements are integral to your overall well-being, ensuring that you possess the energy, resilience, and mental clarity necessary to pursue your long-term goals.

Physical health is maintained through regular exercise, a balanced diet, and sufficient rest, providing the necessary energy and vitality to pursue long-term goals. A healthy body contributes to increased resilience, sharper cognitive function, and an overall sense of well-being.

Sleep plays a pivotal role in physical health, serving as a cornerstone for repair, rejuvenation, and the processing of daily events. A consistent sleep schedule, with adequate hours of rest, is crucial for maintaining optimal physical and mental functioning.

The value of sleep appears to be underestimated by both young and older individuals. For instance, our college-aged teenager often sacrifices sleep by staying up late with friends or spending time on social media. While he claims to be refreshed with a shorter night's sleep, I believe that adopting a more consistent and longer sleep schedule could significantly enhance his ability to process new information efficiently in school and reduce his reliance on stimulants like coffee or energy drinks.

This insight applies to mature individuals as well, particularly those engaged in long and stressful jobs who may survive on limited sleep. Reflecting on my past, I used to be one of those individuals. However, adopting a consistent sleep routine of 7-8 hours per night has led to increased energy, improved mood, and enhanced daily performance. Following my body's natural chronotype and maintaining a consistent bedtime has further contributed to positive changes in energy levels, mood, and overall activity.

The emergence of various technologies and wearable devices has offered individuals tools to monitor sleep patterns, assess sleep quality, and track overall health. Notable sleep technologies include:

1. **Oura Ring:** The Oura Ring is a wearable smart ring equipped with sensors that track sleep patterns, including duration, quality, and stages of sleep (such as deep and REM sleep). It also monitors heart rate, body temperature, and activity levels to provide insights into overall health and recovery.

[Personal Note: I first learned about the Oura Ring a couple of years ago while listening to Tony

Robbins' audiobook *Life Force* while riding my stationary bike. After purchasing my Oura Ring and using it consistently for the last couple of years, I can attest to the uncanny manner in which it can detect any sleep inconsistencies, gauge the quality of my sleep, my readiness level for the next day, and the like. I love it so much I confess I am addicted to it!]

2. **Fitbit and Garmin Watches:** These popular smartwatches offer sleep-tracking features that monitor sleep stages, heart rate, and movement during the night. They provide detailed sleep analysis and personalized insights for improving sleep quality.

3. **Apple Watch:** The Apple Watch provides sleep-tracking capabilities and integrates with the Apple Health app to monitor sleep duration and schedule. It tracks movement during sleep, heart rate, and overall trends to provide sleep analysis and recommendations for better sleep routines.

4. **Whoop Strap:** The Whoop Strap is designed for fitness enthusiasts and athletes, monitoring not only sleep but also recovery metrics such as heart rate variability, respiratory rate, and overall strain on the body, offering insights to optimize training and recovery.

5. **SleepScore Max:** This is a non-wearable sleep tracker that uses a contactless sensor to monitor sleep patterns and quality. Placed on a bedside table, it uses bio-motion sensors to measure sleep without the need to wear any device, providing insights and advice for improved sleep.

6. **Emfit QS Under Mattress Sensor:** This sensor is placed under the mattress to monitor sleep patterns, including sleep stages, heart rate, and breathing rate. It provides detailed sleep analysis without requiring the user to wear any device during sleep.

These devices use a combination of accelerometers, heart rate sensors, and other biometric data to monitor sleep habits and provide users with detailed analyses and recommendations for improving sleep quality and overall health. The devices are capable of tracking sleep duration, quality, and disruptions, offering valuable insights to users for adjusting their sleep routines and promoting better health and well-being.

Diet has a pivotal role in physical health, as a well-balanced diet supplies the essential nutrients crucial for supporting both physical and mental well-being. It has a profound impact on energy levels, mood, and overall vitality. Recognizing nutrition as an investment in long-term health, it's essential to understand how the foods we consume contribute to our well-being. Here are some specific ways in which diet influences physical health:

1. **Nutrient Intake:** A balanced diet ensures the intake of essential nutrients, including vitamins, minerals, carbohydrates, proteins, and fats. These nutrients support bodily functions, such as immune system function, tissue repair, and metabolism.

2. **Weight Management:** Diet impacts body weight and composition. Consuming excess calories can lead to weight gain, while a calorie deficit can lead to weight loss. Maintaining a healthy weight is crucial for overall health and reduces the risk of obesity-related conditions like diabetes and heart disease.

3. **Heart Health:** A diet high in saturated and trans fats, salt, and added sugars can contribute to heart disease. On the other hand, diets rich in fruits, vegetables, whole grains, and healthy fats (like those found in fish and nuts) can support heart health.

4. **Blood Pressure:** Excessive sodium intake, often found in processed foods, can lead to high blood pressure. A diet low in sodium and high in potassium (found in foods like bananas and spinach) can help regulate blood pressure.

5. **Blood Sugar Control:** Carbohydrates in the diet impact blood sugar levels. Monitoring the intake of refined carbohydrates and sugar can help manage blood sugar and reduce the risk of type 2 diabetes.

6. **Digestive Health:** A diet high in fiber, such as that found in whole grains, fruits, and vegetables, supports digestive health by preventing constipation and promoting a balanced gut microbiome.

7. **Bone Health:** Adequate intake of calcium and vitamin D is essential for bone health. Low-fat dairy products, leafy greens, and fortified foods are good sources of these nutrients.

General Diet Recommendations for the Average Person

For the average person, adopting a balanced and nutritious diet can have a profound impact on overall physical health. Here are some general dietary recommendations:

1. **Emphasize Fruits and Vegetables:** Aim to fill half your plate with a variety of fruits and vegetables. They provide essential vitamins, minerals, fiber, and antioxidants.

2. **Choose Whole Grains:** Choose whole grains such as brown rice, whole wheat bread, and quinoa instead of refined grains. They offer more nutrients and fiber.

3. **Include Lean Protein Sources:** Incorporate lean proteins such as poultry, fish, legumes, and tofu into your diet. Limit red meat consumption and opt for lean cuts.

4. **Healthy Fats:** Choose sources of healthy fats like avocados, olive oil, nuts, and fatty fish (e.g., salmon and mackerel). These fats support heart health.

5. **Limit Added Sugars:** Minimize the consumption of foods and drinks high in added sugars, such as sugary beverages and snacks.

6. **Reduce Sodium:** Be mindful of your sodium intake. Avoid highly processed and salty foods and use herbs and spices for flavor instead of salt.

7. **Hydration:** Drink plenty of water throughout the day. Water is essential for digestion, circulation, and temperature regulation.

8. **Portion Control:** Pay attention to portion sizes to prevent overeating. Use smaller plates and be mindful of portion sizes when dining out.

9. **Balanced Meals:** Aim for balanced meals that include a mix of carbohydrates, proteins, and fats. This balance helps stabilize blood sugar levels and provides sustained energy.

10. **Mindful Eating:** Practice mindful eating by savoring your food, paying attention to hunger and fullness cues, and avoiding distractions like screens during meals.

Individual dietary needs vary based on factors like age, activity level, and specific health concerns. For personalized guidance on dietary choices to support optimal physical health, consulting with a healthcare professional or registered dietitian is recommended.

Exercise is a vital component of maintaining and enhancing physical health. It not only strengthens the body but also positively impacts various aspects of well-being. Here are some ways exercise plays an important role in physical health:

1. **Cardiovascular Health:** Exercise strengthens the heart and improves circulation, reducing the risk of heart disease, high blood pressure, and stroke.

2. **Weight Management:** Physical activity helps control body weight by burning calories and maintaining a healthy balance between energy intake and expenditure.

3. **Muscle Strength and Endurance:** Regular exercise, especially resistance training, increases muscle mass and endurance, enhancing overall strength and functional fitness.

4. **Bone Health:** Weight-bearing exercises promote bone density, reducing the risk of osteoporosis.

5. **Metabolism:** Exercise boosts metabolism, helping the body burn calories more efficiently and maintain a healthy body composition.

6. **Mental Health:** Physical activity releases endorphins, reducing stress, improving mood, and alleviating symptoms of anxiety and depression.

7. **Sleep Quality:** Regular exercise can enhance sleep quality, making it easier to fall asleep and stay asleep.

8. **Joint Health:** Exercise helps maintain joint flexibility and reduces the risk of joint-related issues.

9. **Diabetes Management:** Physical activity improves insulin sensitivity and blood sugar control, reducing the risk of type 2 diabetes and assisting in diabetes management.

General Exercise Recommendations for the Average Person

1. **Aerobic Exercise:** Aim for at least 150 minutes of moderate-intensity aerobic exercise or seventy-five minutes of vigorous-intensity aerobic exercise per week.

2. **Strength Training:** Include strength training exercises at least two days a week, focusing on major muscle groups.

3. **Flexibility:** Incorporate flexibility exercises to improve joint mobility, such as stretching or practising yoga.

4. **Balance Training:** Include balance training exercises to prevent falls and improve stability.

5. **Progressive Overload:** Gradually increase the intensity and duration of workouts for continued progress.

6. **Variety:** Include a variety of exercises to work different muscle groups and reduce the risk of overuse injuries.

7. **Safety:** Prioritize safety by using proper form and technique, especially for newcomers or those with specific health concerns.

8. **Consistency:** Establish a consistent exercise routine for long-term benefits.

9. **Listen to Your Body:** Pay attention to your body's signals and modify or rest as needed if you experience pain or discomfort.

10. **Hydration and Nutrition:** Stay well-hydrated and consume a balanced diet to support your exercise routine and overall health.

For those with medical conditions or concerns, consulting a healthcare professional or fitness expert is advisable for personalized exercise recommendations.

Spiritual health involves nurturing values, beliefs, and a sense of purpose, contributing to emotional resilience. General recommendations for nurturing spiritual health include:

1. **Self-Reflection:** Take time for self-reflection and introspection, assessing values, beliefs, and the things that bring meaning to life.

2. **Mindfulness and Meditation:** Practice mindfulness and meditation to connect with the inner self, reduce stress, and foster a deeper understanding.

3. **Connection with Nature:** Spend time in nature to reconnect with the natural world, finding tranquility and spiritual connection.

4. **Cultivate Gratitude:** Practice gratitude by acknowledging positive aspects of life, and expressing appreciation for joy and meaning.

5. **Acts of Kindness:** Engage in acts of kindness and service to others for a sense of fulfillment and spiritual growth.

6. **Engage in Spiritual Practices:** Explore and engage in spiritual practices such as prayer, meditation, yoga, or attending religious services.

7. **Connect with a Community:** Join a spiritual or community group for support and a sense of belonging.

8. **Read and Reflect:** Read spiritual and philosophical texts, reflecting on wisdom shared and its application in life.

9. **Set Intentions:** Set positive intentions for the day or specific situations, staying focused on values and purpose.

10. **Art and Creativity:** Engage in creative activities like art, music, or writing for profound self-connection.

11. **Forgiveness:** Practice forgiveness for emotional healing and spiritual growth.

12. **Mind-Body Connection:** Recognize the connection between physical and spiritual health, nourishing the body to support the spiritual journey.

13. **Seek Guidance:** If struggling with spiritual health or significant life challenges, seek guidance from spiritual leaders, counselors, or therapists.

14. **Maintain an Open Mind:** Be open to exploring different spiritual perspectives for tolerance and understanding.

15. **Celebrate Rituals and Traditions:** Participate in rituals or traditions that hold significance for spiritual journey continuity.

Remember, a balance between physical and spiritual health is crucial for overall well-being. Regularly nurturing both aspects empowers individuals to make informed decisions, leading to optimal health and self-improvement.

"To keep the body in good health is a duty... otherwise, we shall not be able to keep the mind strong and clear."
– Buddha

Buddha's quote eloquently emphasizes the interconnectedness of physical and spiritual health, highlighting that maintaining the body in good health is a duty. The symbiotic relationship between the well-being of the body and the strength and clarity of the mind is underscored. This understanding aligns with the idea that a healthy body provides a foundation for a resilient and clear mind, creating a harmonious balance that contributes to overall well-being.

The Importance of Curiosity

Curiosity is the driving force propelling education and self-improvement forward. Cultivating this quality sets us on a relentless quest for knowledge, understanding, and growth, akin to the boundless wonder of a child exploring the world for the first time.

Children are remarkable models of curiosity, approaching the world with fresh eyes, asking questions, seeking answers, and embracing the unknown with enthusiasm. Their unbridled and limitless curiosity guides them on a path of constant discovery. I vividly recall my first-born son at the age of ten months studying a photo of my wife and me inside a picture frame, attempting to fathom how he could remove us from within this confined space!

As adults, reigniting the flame of curiosity becomes essential for self-improvement. It serves as the spark that ignites the desire to learn, explore, and grow. Curiosity encourages us to question assumptions, challenge our beliefs, and consistently seek new horizons.

In the pursuit of delayed gratification, curiosity becomes the compass guiding us toward self-improvement. It motivates us to embark on new educational journeys, explore unfamiliar territories, and delve into the depths of knowledge. It ensures that our pursuit of success is not a destination but a lifelong journey.

"Curiosity is the wick in the candle of
learning."
– William Arthur Ward

William Arthur Ward's quote reminds us that curiosity is the spark that ignites the flame of knowledge.

Conclusion

In the grand symphony of life, the most harmonious melodies emerge from the pursuit of knowledge and self-improvement. This chapter underscores that investing in oneself stands as the most valuable and enduring investment, transcending age, experience, and wisdom. The pursuit of knowledge and self-improvement knows no bounds of time or circumstance; it is an ever-present opportunity, an eternal wellspring from which we can draw inspiration and wisdom.

> "The capacity to learn is a gift; the ability to learn is a skill; the willingness to learn is a choice."
> – Brian Herbert

This quote encapsulates the essence of lifelong learning and self-improvement, emphasizing that the pursuit of knowledge is both a gift and a choice.

As we bring this chapter to a close, let's reflect on the essential principles we've explored. The act of investing in oneself, encompassing mental, emotional, spiritual, and financial aspects, illuminates a path toward long-term success and personal growth. Embracing the continuous process of learning and skill acquisition is an acknowledgment that our potential knows no bounds. Devotion to physical and spiritual health ensures we possess the vitality and clarity needed to navigate life's intricate passages. Meanwhile, curiosity, that relentless quest for understanding, serves as the eternal flame guiding us, akin to the unwavering curiosity of a child.

In the pursuit of delayed gratification, we discover that the most profound treasures are not material but rather the knowledge we acquire, the growth we experience, and the values we nurture within. The harmonious melodies of our lives are composed of these investments in ourselves, and the symphony they create is a testament to the enduring power of self-improvement.

Chapter 4

Embracing Self-Discipline – The Art of Achievement

In the journey toward delayed gratification and the achievement of our most profound ambitions, self-discipline stands as the beacon guiding us through the tumultuous waters of temptation, instant reward, and distraction. This chapter serves as an exploration of the pivotal role of self-discipline in navigating the path to success. It underscores the intrinsic relationship between delayed gratification, goal achievement, and the practice of self-discipline, highlighting crucial elements that foster this discipline within ourselves. In the quest for success and the realization of our long-term goals, few attributes are as potent as self-discipline. This chapter delves into the profound significance of self-discipline as it relates to delayed gratification, emphasizing the following key points:

Section 1: Practicing Self-Discipline When Faced with Immediate Rewards

Faced with choices that present immediate rewards but may impede long-term progress, self-discipline emerges as a critical skill. The ability to resist the allure of instant gratification becomes a testament to one's commitment to delayed gratification. It entails a conscious choice to prioritize the future over the present, recognizing that the sacrifice today is an investment in tomorrow.

At the core of self-discipline lies the capacity to resist the pull of immediate gratification. The journey toward success is often marked by choices, some offering instant rewards that, in the long run, hinder progress—mastery of self-discipline distinguishes between succumbing to fleeting pleasures and persisting for the greater goal.

In my life, during high school, I excelled as a baseball pitcher. While the allure of immediate gratification tempted me to pursue a career as a professional baseball player, my commitment to delayed gratification and self-discipline led me to choose a path that offered greater stability and certainty for the long term – focusing on my education to become a medical doctor and surgeon.

Practicing self-discipline involves resisting impulsive actions or decisions that may compromise our long-term vision. It embodies the art of delayed gratification, where we sacrifice the immediate for the enduring and the fleeting for the sustainable.

At the heart of self-discipline is the profound ability to withstand the magnetic pull of immediate gratification, a power exemplified by countless individuals who have achieved remarkable success. To deepen our understanding of this concept, let's journey through real-life examples and glean wisdom from renowned figures that illuminate the art of delayed gratification.

Warren Buffett - The Oracle of Omaha: The world-renowned investor, Warren Buffett, stands as a quintessential example of delayed gratification. Despite accumulating vast wealth, he continues to reside in the same modest house he purchased decades ago and drives an ordinary car. His disciplined approach to investing, marked by patience and a long-term vision, has propelled him to become one of the wealthiest individuals globally. Buffett's famous quote, "The stock market is designed to transfer money from the active to the patient," succinctly underscores the value of delaying immediate rewards for the sake of enduring wealth.

— 66 —

"Discipline is choosing between what you
want now and what you want most."
– Abraham Lincoln

— 99 —

Abraham Lincoln's quote reinforces the essence of self-discipline and delayed gratification as prerequisites for enduring success. It emphasizes the importance of sacrificing immediate pleasures for greater, long-term rewards.

J.K. Rowling - The Author Who Overcame Adversity: Before becoming the celebrated author of the Harry Potter series, J.K. Rowling encountered rejection and hardship. She persisted in her writing, delaying the gratification of publishing until she had crafted a story that would captivate millions. Rowling's journey stands as a testament to the enduring power of delayed gratification.

"Rock bottom became the solid
foundation on which I rebuilt my life."
- J.K. Rowling

"Do not bite at the bait of pleasure till
you know there is no hook beneath it."
- Thomas Jefferson

Thomas Jefferson's quote encapsulates the essence of resisting immediate gratification, reminding us that our true desires, long-term goals, and aspirations should not be compromised for fleeting desires.

In these real-life examples and the wisdom of renowned individuals, we witness the mastery of self-discipline in action. The ability to forgo immediate rewards in favor of enduring success is a trait that distinguishes those who achieve greatness. It is the art of recognizing that the most precious treasures often lie at the end of a patient journey, rather than within the allure of immediate gratification.

Section 2: Pausing for Reflection and Considering Consequences

A crucial aspect of self-discipline is the practice of pausing one's actions and reactions. It entails a deliberate examination of the consequences of one's decisions and actions. This pause provides a moment of reflection, allowing individuals to make choices that align with their long-term goals and desired outcomes.

Self-discipline necessitates a deliberate pause before action, involving a consideration of the ramifications of our choices and recognizing that each decision carries consequences. By meticulously contemplating the outcomes, we empower ourselves to make choices aligned with our ultimate goals.

This conscious decision-making process involves weighing the short-term versus long-term gains or losses and acknowledging the trade-offs of our actions. The practice of self-discipline empowers us to choose the path that best serves our overarching objectives.

Self-discipline serves as the anchor that prevents us from being swept away by the tides of impulse and short-term gain. To grasp its essence, we can turn to real-life examples and the wisdom of notable figures who have demonstrated the profound significance of conscious decision-making and the ramifications of our choices.

Steve Jobs - The Visionary Innovator: The late Steve Jobs, co-founder of Apple Inc., serves as a poignant example of the power of conscious decision-making. Upon his return to Apple in 1997, Jobs made the bold decision to streamline the company's product line, focusing on a few exceptional products. This conscious choice marked a pivotal turning point in Apple's history, ultimately leading to the creation of iconic devices such as the iPhone and iPad. Jobs' deliberate pause and discerning decisions played a transformative role in shaping Apple into the tech giant it is today.

Nelson Mandela - The Champion of Justice: Nelson Mandela's decision to pursue justice and equality through non-violence, despite years of imprisonment, stands as a powerful testament to the conscious decision-making process. Mandela demonstrated an acute awareness of the long-term implications of his choices and willingly acknowledged the sacrifices required for the greater good. His commitment to non-violence and the enduring pursuit of justice underscored the profound impact that conscious decision-making can have on shaping a better future for society.

> "In any moment of decision, the best thing you can do is the right thing, the next best thing is the wrong thing, and the worst thing you can do is nothing."
> – Theodore Roosevelt

Theodore Roosevelt's quote highlights the essence of making conscious decisions, emphasizing that the act of decision-making, even in challenging moments, is a critical step toward progress. Self-discipline, as Roosevelt suggests, enables us to make the right decisions, even when they are not the easiest.

In these real-life examples and the wisdom of distinguished individuals, we find the resonance of self-discipline in conscious decision-making. It is the ability to pause, weigh the potential outcomes, and make choices aligned with our ultimate objectives. This practice empowers us to navigate life's intricate decisions, acknowledging that every choice carries the weight of its consequences. It is the path to making decisions that lead us toward our long-term aspirations, even when immediate gratification beckons.

Section 3: Making Appropriate Choices Aligned with Goals

Self-discipline involves making appropriate choices that align with one's goals and desired outcomes. It requires a conscious effort to avoid distractions and temptations that may lead one astray. By consistently making choices that move in the direction of their aspirations, individuals lay the foundation for long-term success.

Self-discipline goes beyond merely resisting temptations; it's about making appropriate choices in line with our aspirations. Every decision becomes a brick in the foundation of our dreams, influencing our journey toward success.

By aligning choices with our goals, we ensure that our actions reflect our intentions. This alignment serves as a compass, navigating us through the labyrinth of distractions and immediate rewards toward our long-term achievements.

To fully grasp the essence of self-discipline, we can draw inspiration from the real-life experiences of notable individuals who have showcased the power of aligning choices with their aspirations. Complementing these stories, we find wisdom in famous quotes that emphasize the significance of every decision as a building block toward success.

Jeff Bezos - The Visionary Entrepreneur: The journey of Jeff Bezos, the founder of Amazon, serves as a remarkable example of the art of aligning choices with one's aspirations. Bezos envisioned creating the world's largest online retailer, and he meticulously selected every decision that brought him closer to that goal. His conscious choices, such as expanding product offerings and pioneering e-commerce innovations, played a pivotal role in influencing Amazon's transformative growth and success. Bezos's journey underscores the power of intentional decision-making in shaping the trajectory of one's aspirations.

"You are free to choose, but you are not free from the consequence of your choice."
- Ezra Taft Benson

Ezra Taft Benson's quote reminds us that every choice we make carries consequences. Self-discipline is the conscious act of considering these consequences and aligning our decisions with our aspirations. It emphasizes the importance of thoughtful decision-making, recognizing that our choices contribute to the shaping of our future and the realization of our long-term goals.

Michael Jordan - The Basketball Legend: Michael Jordan's commitment to his craft, epitomized by rigorous training and unyielding dedication, stands as a testament to aligning choices with the aspiration to be the best. His conscious decisions and relentless pursuit of excellence were instrumental in his journey to basketball greatness. The alignment of his choices with his aspiration led to six NBA championships and a lasting legacy in the sport, showcasing the profound impact of self-discipline on achieving long-term success.

"The path to success is to take massive, determined action."
- Tony Robbins

Tony Robbins' quote emphasizes that success requires not just any action but determined and purposeful action. It underscores the importance of aligning our choices with our goals to make strides toward success.

In the experiences of these remarkable individuals and the wisdom conveyed through famous quotes, we uncover the profound significance of aligning choices with our aspirations. Self-discipline is not a passive act; it's the conscious selection of each decision to construct the foundation of our dreams. It ensures that every brick we lay in this foundation reflects our intentions and guides us through the labyrinth of life's distractions, ultimately leading us to the triumph of our long-term achievements.

Section 4: The Fire in the Belly - Motivation, Drive, and Desire

The fire in the belly, often referred to as motivation, drive, and desire, is intricately linked with self-discipline. It is the inner force that compels individuals to stay the course, even when faced with challenges. This section explores the synergy between self-discipline and the unrelenting motivation that fuels one's journey to success.

To illuminate the concept of motivation, drive, and desire as the driving forces behind self-discipline, we can delve into the real-life experiences of remarkable individuals who have harnessed their inner drive to achieve their goals. Alongside these stories, we can find resonance in famous quotes that underscore the importance of unwavering commitment and relentless pursuit.

Elon Musk - The Visionary Entrepreneur: Elon Musk's relentless pursuit of his goals, particularly in the space and electric vehicle industries, exemplifies the power of inner drive. Despite encountering numerous setbacks and challenges, Musk's unwavering commitment to revolutionize space travel and sustainable transportation has propelled him forward. His dedication to these long-term goals is a testament to the intrinsic motivation that fuels self-discipline. Musk's journey serves as a compelling real-life example of how inner drive, when paired with self-discipline, can surmount obstacles and lead to transformative achievements.

"The difference between a successful person and others is not a lack of strength, not a lack of knowledge, but rather a lack in will."
– Vince Lombardi

Vince Lombardi's quote emphasizes the pivotal role of inner drive and willpower in achieving success. It underscores that self-discipline, fueled by unwavering commitment, is a distinguishing factor that sets successful individuals apart. Lombardi's words highlight the importance of harnessing the fire in the belly, the motivation that propels individuals to persist in the face of challenges and aligns their actions with their long-term goals.

Serena Williams - The Tennis Champion: Serena Williams' dedication to tennis and her pursuit of greatness is a testament to the power of inner drive. Her burning passion for the sport and her unwavering commitment to excellence have led to numerous Grand Slam titles and a legacy as one of the greatest tennis players in history. Williams' journey exemplifies the profound impact of inner drive on achieving remarkable success, showcasing how a relentless commitment to one's craft can elevate performance to unparalleled heights.

"Desire is the key to motivation, but it's determination and commitment to an unrelenting pursuit of your goal – a commitment to excellence – that will enable you to attain the success you seek."
- Mario Andretti

Mario Andretti's quote encapsulates the relationship between desire, determination, and commitment. It acknowledges that inner drive and a relentless pursuit of goals are vital components of self-discipline that lead to success.

In the experiences of these extraordinary individuals and the wisdom conveyed through famous quotes, we recognize the central role of motivation, drive, and desire in self-discipline. It is this burning passion and unwavering commitment that propel us forward, enabling us to make choices aligned with our long-term goals. This intrinsic motivation serves as a constant reminder of the rewards that await us beyond the allure of immediate gratification, motivating us to practice self-discipline and stay the course on our journey to success.

Section 5: Avoiding Multitasking and Efficient Goal Achievement

Self-discipline involves the ability to avoid multitasking, a practice that can hinder efficient goal achievement. Multitasking not only divides one's focus but also diminishes the quality of work. This section discusses the significance of single-tasking and how it contributes to better self-discipline and goal attainment.

Multitasking, often seen as a badge of productivity, stands in stark contradiction to self-discipline. The perceived efficiency of juggling tasks simultaneously actually dilutes focus, compromises efficiency, and undermines self-discipline.

Section 6: The Neuroscience of Multitasking

Recent neuroscientific research sheds light on the detrimental effects of multitasking on cognitive performance. MRI studies reveal that when people engage in multiple tasks, brain activity becomes divided and less efficient. It's as if the brain attempts to toggle between tasks, resulting in a reduced capacity to focus.

Studies also indicate that multitasking increases the production of the stress hormone cortisol, which can impair memory, attention, and decision-making. It erodes the ability to prioritize tasks and undermines self-discipline.

Moreover, research using functional MRI (fMRI) shows that frequent multitaskers exhibit reduced brain density in areas responsible for cognitive control and emotional regulation. This points to the structural changes that can occur as a consequence of persistent multitasking.

In essence, neuroscience unveils the paradox of multitasking: while it may seem like an efficient way to manage multiple tasks, it dilutes focus, compromises efficiency, and erodes self-discipline. The brain's limited ability to truly focus on more than one task at a time leads to decreased productivity, more errors, and increased stress. In the symphony of self-discipline, avoiding the siren call of multitasking is the melody that allows us to harmonize our efforts and stay on course towards our long-term objectives.

Multitasking, commonly perceived as a symbol of productivity, deserves deeper scrutiny through the lens of neuroscience, supported by real-life examples and renowned quotes that underscore the adverse effects of this practice on productivity and self-discipline.

Bill Gates - The Focus Advocate: Bill Gates, the co-founder of Microsoft and a prolific philanthropist, stands as an advocate for focused work. Despite the demands of his roles, Gates is known for his ability to concentrate on one task at a time. His disciplined approach to work demonstrates that tackling one task with undivided attention often yields better results than juggling multiple tasks simultaneously. Gates' success and productivity serve as a real-life example of the benefits of single-tasking and focused work in achieving meaningful outcomes.

"The art of leadership is saying no, not saying yes. It is very easy to say yes."
- Tony Blair

Tony Blair's quote highlights the art of leadership and decision-making, stressing the importance of selective focus. Multitasking often leads to a lack of discernment in choosing where to direct one's efforts. Blair's insight underscores the value of concentrated attention on key priorities, emphasizing the need for leaders to make discerning decisions and avoid the pitfalls of spreading oneself too thin through multitasking.

Tim Ferriss - The Productivity Expert: Tim Ferriss, the author of *The 4-Hour Workweek* and a well-known productivity guru, emphasizes the dangers of multitasking. He conducted an experiment in which he intentionally avoided checking his email first thing in the morning, instead focusing on a single critical task. This approach significantly improved his productivity and efficiency. Ferriss' experience illustrates the impact of prioritizing focused work over multitasking. It reinforces the idea that concentrating on a singular, important task can lead to better outcomes and increased efficiency, aligning with the principles of self-discipline and goal attainment.

"The most important thing in
communication is hearing what isn't said."
– Peter Drucker

Peter Drucker's quote underscores the significance of active listening and undivided attention. In the context of multitasking, attempting to listen while simultaneously engaging in other tasks can result in crucial information being overlooked or misunderstood. This quote highlights the communication challenges that can arise from attempting to juggle multiple tasks and the importance of focused attention in effective communication.

In the pursuit of self-discipline and success, the practice of multitasking emerges as a double-edged sword. While often celebrated as a symbol of productivity, multitasking, when scrutinized through the lenses of real-life examples, famous quotes, and neuroscience, reveals its pernicious effects. The unwavering commitment and focused attention of visionary individuals such as Bill Gates and Tim Ferriss highlight the superiority of single-tasking in the realm of goal achievement.

These renowned quotes underscore the value of passion and selective focus in achieving greatness, while also emphasizing the importance of discernment and leadership. Moreover, neuroscience provides compelling evidence that multitasking divides cognitive resources, compromises efficiency, and weakens self-discipline. This neurological perspective exposes the paradox of multitasking: an illusion of productivity that ultimately diminishes focus, increases errors, and heightens stress. In the symphony of self-discipline, the melody of selective and focused work harmonizes our efforts and steers us closer to our long-term aspirations, away from the cacophony of multitasking distractions.

Section 7: The Importance of Focus and Communication

Focus and effective communication are instrumental in mastering self-discipline and achieving ultimate goals and successes. This section explores how maintaining focus and clear communication enhances the practice of self-discipline, facilitating the alignment of efforts toward long-term objectives. I would argue that this singular focus exercised by self-discipline is indeed the positive connotation of the term "obsession". Although obsession is generally referred to by its negative connotation of a persistent and intrusive preoccupation regarding an idea or activity, I would choose to shift the paradigm and tell you that obsession is a laser-like focus and unwavering commitment, a driving force that propels us toward our goals. This shift in perspective is crucial in understanding how obsession can be a source of resilience, perseverance, and determination.

The importance of focus and effective communication in the realm of self-discipline is underscored by real-life examples and renowned quotes. These principles serve as the cornerstones of achieving our goals, fostering unwavering commitment, and creating an environment conducive to success.

Warren Buffett - The Focused Investor: Warren Buffett, often referred to as the "Oracle of Omaha," is renowned for his extraordinary investment success. Central to his approach is an unyielding focus on a limited number of stocks. His disciplined concentration on a select few investments has yielded remarkable long-term returns, showcasing the power of focus in achieving financial goals. Buffett's strategy highlights how a singular, concentrated focus on a few well-chosen endeavors can lead to significant success and serves as a real-life example of the positive connotation of the term "obsession" when it comes to achieving goals.

"The successful warrior is the average
man, with laser-like focus."
- Bruce Lee

Bruce Lee's quote emphasizes the transformative potential of unwavering focus. It illuminates how channeling our attention singularly towards a task or goal can elevate us from the ordinary to the extraordinary, a vital aspect of self-discipline. Lee's insight underscores the profound impact that a laser-like focus can have on achieving excellence and transcending mediocrity, aligning with the principles of self-discipline and goal attainment.

Martin Luther King Jr. – The Civil Rights Visionary: Martin Luther King Jr.'s leadership in the civil rights movement serves as a profound example of effective communication. His "I Have a Dream" speech resonated with millions and rallied support for the cause. King's ability to articulate a vision and communicate it effectively created a conducive environment for social change. His skillful use of words and compelling communication played a crucial role in inspiring and mobilizing people, showcasing how effective communication is an essential component of leadership and achieving meaningful goals.

"The single biggest problem in
communication is the illusion that it
has taken place."
– George Bernard Shaw

George Bernard Shaw's quote underscores the necessity of effective communication. It reminds us that merely articulating our goals is insufficient; we must ensure that our message is not only conveyed but also comprehended. Misunderstandings or unfulfilled communication can impede self-discipline and the realization of our aspirations.

In these real-life examples and the wisdom of renowned quotes, we find the synergy between focus and effective communication in the context of self-discipline. Focus serves as the guiding force that fortifies our commitment and steers us away from distractions. Effective communication complements this focus, enabling us to articulate our goals clearly and create an environment conducive to achieving them. These principles together lay the foundation for success, allowing us to navigate the complexities of self-discipline and reach our long-term aspirations with greater efficacy and precision.

Section 8: Self-Discipline as the Art of Achievement

Self-discipline is the linchpin that holds together the concept of delayed gratification. It is the singular attribute that empowers individuals to make choices today that ensures a brighter tomorrow. This section brings together the principles discussed throughout the chapter, reinforcing the idea that self-discipline is the catalyst for success.

Conclusion: Harnessing Self-Discipline for Delayed Gratification

In the grand symphony of achievement, self-discipline is the conductor that orchestrates the harmonious progression toward success. It enables individuals to navigate the labyrinth of choices, recognizing that some paths offer immediate rewards while others lead to the realization of long-term goals.

Self-discipline provides the critical pause needed for reflection, a moment in which consequences are carefully weighed and appropriate choices made. It is the unyielding commitment to a vision, the fire in the belly that propels individuals forward in the face of adversity.

This chapter has also shed light on the detriments of multitasking and the neuroscience behind its counterproductive nature. It has underscored the importance of maintaining focus and effective communication as key elements in mastering self-discipline.

As the chapter concludes, it is evident that self-discipline is indeed the superpower to success, the bridge between delayed gratification and the ultimate realization of one's goals and aspirations. With every choice, every moment of reflection, and every focused action, individuals harness the extraordinary power of self-discipline on their journey to enduring success.

Chapter 5

Cultivating Patience - The Key to Delayed Gratification

In a world that increasingly celebrates instant results, the cultivation of patience emerges as a rare and precious virtue. The delayed gratification mindset transcends mere waiting; it embodies the art of patience. This perspective recognizes that success is a journey, not an overnight occurrence. It involves the discerning anticipation of opportune moments, the judicious making of decisions, and the honing of listening skills. This chapter intricately explores the multifaceted realm of patience, unveils the adverse facets of instant gratification in the digital age, and scrutinizes the repercussions of parenting styles that imbue children with a penchant for immediate satisfaction.

Introduction

"Patience is a virtue," they say, and with good reason. In a world defined by instant gratification, the cultivation of patience stands as a crucial element in adopting the delayed gratification mindset. Patience serves as the bedrock of this mindset, representing the capacity to endure and persist, even when the enticement of immediate satisfaction beckons. In a society that places growing emphasis on speed and convenience, patience frequently finds itself relegated to a secondary role. Nevertheless, it is precisely patience that empowers us to attain enduring success and fulfillment in the long term.

In this chapter, we'll delve into the multifaceted nature of patience, unraveling its profound role in shaping the path to success. It examines the importance of patiently waiting for opportune moments and highlights the significance of listening and exercising self-restraint in a world characterized by rapidity. Furthermore, the discussion extends to the detrimental impact of technology and social media, shedding light on their role in promoting instant gratification. Additionally, the chapter scrutinizes the consequences of parents instilling this mentality in their children, creating a comprehensive exploration of patience in the contemporary context.

Section 1: Success is a Journey, Not an Overnight Phenomenon

One of the fundamental aspects of patience lies in recognizing that success is not an instantaneous occurrence; rather, it is an ongoing evolution marked by progress, setbacks, and persistent effort. In a world where instant fame and fortune often dominate headlines, the toil and perseverance behind significant achievements are easily overlooked.

As a freshman high school teenager, I faced a severe case of *acne conglobata*, a condition so intense that it merited publication in medical journals. This ailment led to a "fever of unknown origin," requiring a two-month hospitalization during my freshman year, marked by facial surgeries and skin grafts. Despite the considerable time lost in school, I endeavored to stay engaged with my studies during hospitalization. Upon recovery, the journey to resume school demanded immense patience, perseverance, and determination, culminating in my eventual achievement as the Valedictorian three years later. This narrative serves as a testament to the transformative power of self-discipline, patience, commitment, and unwavering determination, even in the face of embarrassment and ostracization.

Success stories, such as that of Colonel Sanders, the founder of KFC, exemplify the patience required on the path to success. At the age of sixty-five, after numerous rejections, he finally secured a franchisee willing to collaborate, paving the way for the global success of Kentucky Fried Chicken. His journey epitomizes the value of patience, resilience, and steadfast determination in the face of adversity.

Patience is often characterized as a willingness to endure setbacks and delays, recognizing that success is a journey, not an overnight phenomenon. This perspective forms the bedrock of the delayed gratification mindset— an acknowledgment that meaningful achievements necessitate time and effort.

Consider the following:

• **Delayed Gratification as a Long-Term Investment:** Achieving success through delayed gratification is analogous to making a long-term investment. Although it may not yield immediate returns, over time, it can lead to substantial benefits.

"Patience, persistence, and perspiration make
an unbeatable combination for success."
– Napoleon Hill

- **The Myth of Overnight Success:** Many apparent overnight success stories reveal years of hard work and perseverance upon closer examination. The Beatles, for instance, spent countless hours refining their craft in obscurity before achieving global fame.

"The key to everything is patience. You get the chicken by hatching the egg, not by smashing it."
– Arnold H. Glasow

- **The Patience of Visionaries:** Visionaries like Elon Musk and Jeff Bezos serve as prime examples of individuals exhibiting unwavering patience in the pursuit of ambitious goals. Ventures such as SpaceX and Amazon required immense patience to overcome challenges and emerge as industry leaders.

"Success is not final, failure is not fatal: It is
the courage to continue that counts."
– Winston Churchill

Section 2: Waiting for the Right Opportunities and Making Thoughtful Decisions

Patience, far from being a passive waiting, embodies an active and discerning waiting. It involves the astuteness to recognize opportune moments and the wisdom to exercise restraint. Hastily rushing into decisions or actions may yield instant gratification but often comes at the expense of sacrificing long-term goals.

Warren Buffett, a paragon of success in the investment world, epitomizes this principle. His investment philosophy revolves around the virtues of patience and thoughtful decision-making. He succinctly captured this ethos when he declared, "The stock market is designed to transfer money from the Active to the Patient." His remarkable success is attributed to his ability to patiently await the right investment opportunities, steadfastly resisting the allure of impulsive decisions that ensnare others.

Patience, as a virtue, extends beyond enduring delays; it involves waiting for opportune moments and making deliberate decisions. Impulsivity, on the other hand, can result in costly mistakes, whereas patience enables the seizing of the right moments. Consider the following aspects:

- The Art of Timing: Waiting for the opportune moment can be the differentiator between success and failure. Entrepreneurs, for instance, often wait for ideal market conditions before launching new products or services.
- Strategic Decision-Making: Successful leaders and decision-makers comprehend the value of patience in strategic planning. They meticulously assess options and patiently await the optimal course of action.

— 66 —————————

"Opportunities come infrequently.
When it rains gold, put out the bucket,
not the thimble."
– Warren Buffett

————————— 99 —

- **Resisting Pressure:** In a society that frequently glorifies immediate results, the ability to resist external pressure and adhere to a long-term vision becomes a hallmark of patience. Warren Buffett's patient approach to stock market investments is a prime example.

"Trees that are slow to grow bear the best fruit."
– Molière

Section 3: Developing Listening Skills

Patience extends beyond waiting for external factors; it also encompasses inner stillness and the ability to truly listen. In a world where everyone appears eager to be the dominant voice in the room, those who master the art of patient listening often gain deeper insights and make more informed choices.

- **Active Listening:** Active listening is a patient and empathetic form of engagement where one fully absorbs the speaker's words, emotions, and intentions. This skill has the potential to enhance both personal and professional relationships.

"The most basic of all human needs is the
need to understand and be understood.
The best way to understand people is to
listen to them." – Ralph G. Nichols

- **Cultivating Empathy:** Patience fosters empathy, enabling a better understanding of the perspectives and experiences of others. This, in turn, leads to improved communication, conflict resolution, and collaboration.

"To listen well is as powerful a means of
communication and influence as to talk well."
– John Marshall

- **Leadership and Patience:** Effective leaders are often those who practice patient listening. They establish inclusive environments where every voice is valued, resulting in innovative solutions and motivated teams.

"Most people do not listen with the intent
to understand; they listen with the intent
to reply."
– Stephen R. Covey

The great philosopher Søren Kierkegaard once said, "Patience is necessary, and one cannot reap immediately where one has sown." This quote underscores the idea that patience involves allowing ideas and perspectives to flourish, letting conversations develop, and learning from others. It's about giving others the space and time to express themselves.

A noteworthy example from my thirty-five years in medical practice involves my commitment to actively listening to my patients. Rather than rushing through examinations to attend to the next patient, I adhere to a personal clinic model. In this approach, I establish rapport with each patient, learning about their background and often inquiring about their current or former occupation. By listening attentively, I create a bond of friendship that allows me to make personalized medical recommendations. In fact, my tenured staff recognizes my clinic tagline: "I am an actor on stage," presenting a scene where my full and undivided attention is dedicated solely to the patient in front of me. I eliminate any distractions in my life, both personal and professional, devoting my full energy and attention to the patients and their needs.

Section 4: The Negative Attributes of Social Media and Technology

In today's digitally connected world, social media and technology have significantly heightened the demand for instant gratification. The incessant flow of notifications, likes, and shares has conditioned individuals to seek immediate rewards, leaving little room for the patience inherent in a delayed gratification mindset.

Social media platforms, designed to maintain user engagement and deliver swift feedback, contribute to a constant need for validation and a fear of missing out. The relentless pursuit of instant gratification through social media often comes at the expense of authentic connections and real-world experiences. While the digital age has brought unparalleled convenience and immediacy, it has also accentuated the negative aspects of instant gratification:

• **Information Overload:** The continuous influx of information from social media, news, and the internet can foster impatience. Accustomed to instant updates and immediate responses, individuals may overlook the importance of the experience created by technology.

"The technology you use impresses no one. The experience you create with it is everything."
– Sean Gerety

- **Distracted Minds:** Technology encourages multitasking and continuous partial attention, eroding our ability to focus and cultivate patience. Restless minds easily succumb to distractions, hindering critical thinking. Thinking critically allows for a deeper understanding of issues, enabling more informed decisions and responses.

"The instant gratification of the digital age has made patience almost obsolete."
– Stuart Appley

• **Comparison Culture:** Social media often presents idealized versions of people's lives, fostering unrealistic expectations and a "keeping up with the Joneses" mentality. Patience becomes a scarce commodity in this culture of constant comparison. In a personal example, my wife and I, with our son's approval, opted for a private boarding school for our eldest. However, the comparison culture in the school, dominated by wealthy families, adversely affected our son's self-esteem. The experience highlighted the detrimental impact of instant gratification and the importance of fostering patience.

• **Validation-Seeking Behavior:** Instant likes, shares, and comments on social media platforms create a craving for immediate validation. This can lead to impulsive behaviors and diminished patience, as emphasized by Alysia Harris: "The moment you feel like you have to prove your worth to someone is the moment to absolutely and utterly walk away."

Section 5: Parents and Instant Gratification

How we raise our children significantly influences their understanding of patience, with parents playing a pivotal role in instilling values, including their attitude towards instant gratification. In certain instances, parents may inadvertently contribute to the instant gratification mindset by readily providing their children with everything they desire without merit or effort. This can lead to entitlement and a lack of appreciation for hard work and patience. Conversely, parents who emphasize the value of patience, effort, and delayed gratification empower their children to navigate life's challenges with resilience.

Parents shape their children's approach to patience and gratification in several ways:

• **Overindulgence:** Parents who fulfill every desire of their children without requiring merit or effort may instil a sense of entitlement and instant gratification. Children may grow up expecting immediate rewards without grasping the value of patience.

• **Delayed Consequences:** Shielding children from the consequences of their actions can deprive them of crucial life lessons. Allowing them to experience setbacks and learn from their mistakes fosters patience and resilience.

• **Teaching Delayed Gratification:** Parents can impart the importance of patience by teaching children to set goals, work towards them, and understand that success often requires time and perseverance.

• **Role Modeling:** Children learn by observing their parents. Parents who model patience, resilience, and delayed gratification are more likely to instill these values in their children.

"The greatest gifts you can give your
children are the roots of responsibility
and the wings of independence."
- Denis Waitley

Section 6: The Importance of Patience

Patience is a virtue that empowers individuals to overcome obstacles, make informed decisions, and endure the uncertainties of life. It forms the bedrock of the delayed gratification mindset, allowing individuals to stay focused on long-term goals despite the allure of instant rewards. Patience stands as the antithesis of impulsivity, fostering wisdom, resilience, and a deeper understanding of the world.

"Patience and perseverance have a magical
effect before which difficulties disappear
and obstacles vanish."
– John Quincy Adams

In the words of Victor Hugo, "Even the darkest night will end, and the sun will rise." This quote encapsulates the essence of patience. No matter how challenging the journey, patience allows us to endure and believe in the promise of a new day. It reminds us that success is not a sprint but a marathon, and the ability to cultivate patience is the torch that guides us through the darkest nights toward the dawn of our dreams.

Conclusion

The art of cultivating patience is a skill that requires consistent practice and unwavering dedication. It involves recognizing that success is a journey rather than an instantaneous phenomenon. The capacity to patiently await opportune moments, make thoughtful decisions, and hone one's listening skills is crucial. In a world shaped by the potentially detrimental aspects of social media and technology, and influenced by diverse parenting styles, patience emerges as a formidable superpower.

Patience serves as the bridge connecting individuals to the mindset of delayed gratification, guiding them towards the fulfillment of long-term goals and aspirations. In its profound simplicity, patience stands as the cornerstone of the journey towards delayed gratification.

"Have patience. All things are difficult before they become easy."
– Saadi

Chapter 6

The Art of Avoiding Impulsive Decisions in Mastering Delayed Gratification

In our fast-paced contemporary world, where instant gratification is exalted, and impulsive decisions are often mistaken for assertiveness, the ability to resist the allure of short-term pleasures becomes a formidable superpower. This chapter delves into the profound importance of eschewing impulsive decisions, advocating for a strategic pause that allows the initial rush of desire to dissipate. By pausing and revisiting decisions after a period of contemplation, individuals can navigate the intricacies of delayed gratification, steering their course towards long-term success and fulfillment. This chapter emphasizes the significance of pausing, allowing impulsive decisions to marinate in the subconscious mind, and revisiting them with a clearer perspective after the initial urge has faded.

"Think of many things; do one."
– Portuguese Proverb

Understanding the Impulse:

Impulsive decisions often stem from the immediate desire for gratification without a thorough consideration of the long-term consequences. In a society that values quick results, the concept of pausing to avoid impulsivity challenges the norm. It invites individuals to embrace the discomfort of delay, recognizing that true satisfaction is often found in the patience to wait for a more substantial reward.

The impulse is a powerful force rooted in the brain's complex interplay of emotions, desires, and the pursuit of pleasure. It often drives us to seek immediate rewards, and in the process, we may overlook the long-term consequences of our actions. The concept of avoiding impulsive decisions is not about denying ourselves joy or satisfaction but rather about ensuring that our choices align with our broader objectives.

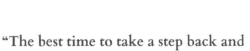

"The best time to take a step back and reevaluate is when you're feeling overwhelmed and impulsive."
– Anonymous

The Power of the Pause:

When faced with the temptation of impulsive decisions, the act of pausing serves as a powerful intervention. It introduces a temporal gap between the initial impulse and the subsequent action, allowing the individual to reassess their priorities and goals. The pause provides a critical breathing space, enabling a more thoughtful and rational evaluation of the situation.

The simple act of pausing when faced with impulsive decisions is akin to hitting the reset button on our decision-making process. It provides a crucial buffer, disrupting the automatic response pattern that often leads to impulsive actions. This pause allows time for the initial emotional charge to dissipate, creating space for rational thought and a more objective evaluation of the situation.

When we pause, we interrupt the momentum of impulsivity, creating a mental space that fosters self-reflection. This intentional delay acts as a natural filter, separating momentary desires from enduring values and long-term goals. It is in this intermission that the seeds of delayed gratification are sown.

"Patience, persistence, and perspiration make
an unbeatable combination for success."
- Napoleon Hill

Letting Impulses Settle in the Subconscious:

The subconscious mind plays a pivotal role in decision-making. Allowing impulsive decisions to sink into the subconscious mind is a strategic move in the chess game of decision-making. This process involves acknowledging the impulse without acting on it immediately. Instead, we let it simmer below the surface, giving our subconscious mind time to process the emotional charge and separate it from the rational assessment of our goals. This process facilitates a gradual dissipation of the immediate urge, creating an environment where rational thinking can prevail over impulsive tendencies.

By letting impulsive decisions sink in, we engage in a form of mental incubation. This incubation period is where the initial allure of instant gratification undergoes scrutiny. It provides an opportunity for the subconscious mind to consider the long-term consequences, potential risks, and alignment with our overarching objectives.

"A moment of patience in a moment of anger saves you a hundred moments of regret."
– Anonymous

The One-Week Revisit:

Revisiting impulsive decisions after a week or more is a strategic approach to decision-making. The passage of time allows for a shift in perspective and a reduction in the emotional charge associated with the initial impulse. This reflective period empowers individuals to make decisions from a more balanced and informed standpoint, aligning their choices with long-term goals rather than succumbing to fleeting desires.

The beauty of delaying decisions is evident when we revisit them after the initial impulsive urge has faded. What once seemed like an irresistible temptation may now be viewed with a more discerning eye. This clarity stems from the dissipation of the "momentary high" that often clouds judgment in the heat of the moment.

Revisiting decisions with a clear mind allows us to evaluate them in the context of our long-term goals. It unveils a perspective that was temporarily obscured by the immediate desire for gratification. In this renewed light, we can make decisions that align with our values and contribute to our overarching success.

A pertinent example that comes to mind as I write this chapter is that currently my family and I are in an all-inclusive fancy resort in Cancun, Mexico. Upon check-in, the protocol for the resort is to meet with a representative who discusses and urges each family to schedule a free, no-obligation "presentation" in the next day or two. During this presentation, the main hotel in the resort takes you by shuttle to an even fancier hotel about five minutes away to give you a wonderful free breakfast while at the same time showing you a ninety-minute presentation, including a tour, of the brand-new hotel located within the same vast resort complex.

Once we arrive there and have breakfast with the initial representative, it quickly becomes apparent that the entire goal is to sell the resort guests on a variety of memberships with different levels of service. As I start asking too many questions and do not immediately purchase, a different higher-level representative takes over. This process continues through an additional three representatives, all the while gradually lowering the membership initiation fee, increasing the number of future free rooms, and even offering ten-year no-interest financing on purchasing the membership.

Although the concept and terms seem alluring, the actual fixed cost is more than an average monthly mortgage payment for most Americans for a period of ten years, with a percent initial down payment. If it were not for my wife, who quickly put her foot down to hit the "pause" button, our kids would have loved for us to purchase this membership…after all, it undoubtedly is a phenomenal resort with beautiful amenities, numerous high-end restaurants, wonderful daytime activities, and nighttime entertainment. This ability, demonstrated beautifully by my wife, to delay impulsive decisions and to revisit it again seven to ten days later was a game-changer. Here I now sit ten days later, and I realize that committing to such an exorbitant long-term financial decision in the heat of the moment would have been an extraordinarily grave and erroneous decision.

"Rivers know this: There is no hurry.
We shall get there someday."
- A.A. Milne, from Winnie the Pooh

The quotes highlighted above underscore the wisdom of pausing, reflecting, and avoiding impulsive decisions. They emphasize the importance of patience and the long-lasting impact of thoughtful choices over hasty actions. In the realm of delayed gratification, these quotes serve as reminders that the journey to success is paved with careful consideration and strategic decision-making.

The Importance of This Concept in Achieving Goals:

1. **Alignment with Long-Term Goals:** The concept of avoiding impulsive decisions aligns seamlessly with the pursuit of long-term goals. Success is often the culmination of a series of deliberate and well-thought-out choices. By resisting the urge for instant gratification, individuals ensure that their decisions contribute positively to their overarching objectives.

2. **Enhanced Decision-Making:** The ability to pause and revisit decisions bolsters the decision-making process. It fosters clarity and sound judgment, reducing

the likelihood of making choices driven solely by momentary desires. This enhanced decision-making capacity is a cornerstone of goal achievement.

3. **Building Resilience:** Avoiding impulsive decisions cultivates resilience. It reinforces the idea that setbacks or delays in gratification are not obstacles but rather growth opportunities. Resilience becomes a key trait that propels individuals forward in the face of challenges, ensuring they stay committed to their goals.

Real-Time Examples:

1. Financial Investments:

- *Impulse #1:* A sudden desire to invest in a volatile stock due to a friend's success.

- *Pause and Revisit:* After a week, upon reconsideration and consulting financial advisors, the investor realizes the high risk and decides to opt for a more stable and strategic investment.

- *Impulse #2:* Imagine you come across an enticing online sale for an item you've been eyeing.

- *Pause and Revisit:* Instead of impulsively clicking "buy," you pause, letting the desire sink in. A week later, the urgency has waned, and you realize that the purchase doesn't align with your financial goals.

2. Career Transitions:

- *Impulse #1:* Deciding to quit a job impulsively due to a challenging day.
- *Pause and Revisit:* Taking a week to reflect on the long-term career goals, the individual realizes that the current challenges are temporary and opts to stay while actively seeking solutions to improve the work environment.
- *Impulse #2:* Faced with a tempting job offer that promises immediate perks but may disrupt your long-term career trajectory, you decide to let the offer sink in.
- *Pause and Revisit:* After a period of reflection, you realize that staying on your current path aligns better with your professional aspirations. Remember, the grass is not always greener on the other side.

3. Personal Relationships:

- *Impulse #1:* Agreeing to a major personal commitment impulsively in the excitement of the moment.
- *Pause and Revisit:* After a week of contemplation, the individual realizes the magnitude of the commitment and decides to communicate openly about their reservations, ensuring a more informed and consensual decision.

- *Impulse #2:* In the heat of an argument, you feel the impulse to send a strongly worded message.
- *Pause and Revisit:* Instead, you decide to pause and let the emotion sink in. Days later, you revisit the situation with a cooler head and choose a more constructive approach to resolve the conflict.

In the pursuit of delayed gratification and ultimate success, the art of avoiding impulsive decisions emerges as a critical skill. The intentional pause, allowing impulses to sink into the subconscious mind, and revisiting decisions with clarity form a dynamic process that aligns our actions with our long-term goals. As we navigate the complex landscape of desires and decisions, mastering this art becomes a superpower, empowering us to make choices that stand the test of time and contribute to enduring success.

Chapter 7

The Resilience Paradox: Building Strengths through Setbacks

Resilience, the ability to bounce back from adversity, stands as a cornerstone in the delayed gratification journey. In this chapter, we'll explore the profound role resilience plays in the pursuit of delayed gratification, viewing setbacks as opportunities for growth, overcoming obstacles as integral to the journey, embracing failure, and harnessing criticism to fuel passion. As we navigate the complexities of delayed gratification, resilience emerges as a potent force that not only propels us through challenges but transforms setbacks into steppingstones toward long-term success.

"Perseverance is not a long race; it's
many short races one after another."
– Walter Elliot

Resilience: A Pillar of Delayed Gratification

At the heart of delayed gratification lies the understanding that the path to success is often strewn with challenges, setbacks, and moments of doubt. Resilience, the capacity to endure and adapt in the face of adversity, becomes a guiding force. Rather than viewing obstacles as insurmountable roadblocks, individuals on the delayed gratification journey see them as opportunities for resilience to shine.

"Resilience is the symphony that plays
in the aftermath of setbacks, turning
discord into a melody of growth."
– Anonymous

The Resilience Paradox: Turning Setbacks into Springboards

Setbacks, obstacles, and challenges are not detours on the road to success but rather integral components of the journey. The resilience paradox lies in the ability to not only endure these difficulties but to leverage them as opportunities for growth. It involves a mindset shift where setbacks are reframed as springboards for greater achievements. Instead of viewing challenges as roadblocks, individuals on the delayed gratification journey see them as opportunities to test and strengthen their resilience.

"In the tapestry of success, setbacks are the threads that weave resilience, creating a fabric that withstands the test of time."
- Anonymous

Viewing Setbacks as Opportunities:

1. **Growth Mindset:** Resilient individuals approach setbacks with a growth mindset. Instead of seeing failure as a dead-end, they view it as a detour on the road to success. The setbacks become opportunities for learning, adaptation, and personal growth.

2. **Learning from Adversity:** Every setback carries lessons. Resilience involves extracting wisdom from challenges, understanding the nuances of what went wrong, and leveraging that knowledge to make more informed decisions in the future. Each setback is a classroom where delayed gratification is both tested and refined.

3. **Building Emotional Stamina:** Resilience is not just about bouncing back; it's about enduring the emotional toll of setbacks. By viewing challenges as opportunities, individuals develop emotional stamina. They learn to navigate the waves of disappointment, frustration, and uncertainty that often accompany delayed gratification.

4. **Overcoming Obstacles: The Steppingstones of Delayed Gratification:** Obstacles are not impediments to success but rather steppingstones that propel individuals forward on the path of delayed gratification. The journey is seldom linear; it weaves through peaks and valleys, presenting hurdles that demand perseverance. Each obstacle surmounted becomes a testament to one's resilience and a foundation for future success. In the delayed gratification mindset, individuals embrace obstacles as crucial components of their journey, understanding that overcoming challenges leads to long-term growth. The process of navigating obstacles fosters

adaptability, resourcefulness, and a deeper understanding of oneself.

— 66 ——

"Obstacles are not roadblocks; they are
the stones we step on to reach the
summit of delayed gratification."
- Anonymous

—— 99 —

Overcoming Obstacles - A Crucial Element of the Journey:

- **Obstacles as Growth Catalysts:** The delayed gratification journey is inherently challenging, with obstacles serving as catalysts for personal and professional growth. Overcoming these hurdles is not just a byproduct; it's an integral part of the journey itself. Each obstacle conquered contributes to the resilience reservoir.

- **Strength in Adversity:** The ability to overcome obstacles builds a unique strength that becomes a defining characteristic on the path to delayed gratification. It's not about avoiding challenges but confronting them head-on and emerging stronger on the other side.

> "It's not whether you get knocked down,
> it's whether you get up."
> – Vince Lombardi

- **Long-Term Vision:** Resilience is fueled by a long-term vision. Individuals on the delayed gratification journey understand that enduring short-term discomfort and overcoming obstacles pave the way for enduring success. Each challenge is a mile marker on the road to delayed but deeply satisfying gratification.

> "It is really wonderful how much resilience
> there is in human nature. Let any obstructing
> cause, no matter what, be removed in any way,
> even by death, and we fly back to first
> principles of hope and enjoyment."
> – Bram Stoker

Embracing Failure as a Teacher

Failure is not the end but a critical juncture in the delayed gratification journey. Embracing failure as a teacher, rather than a verdict, is essential to developing resilience. Failures offer valuable lessons, insights, and opportunities for improvement. Those on the path of delayed gratification recognize that setbacks are not synonymous with defeat but rather steppingstones toward eventual success.

The ability to dissect failure, extract lessons, and apply newfound knowledge is a hallmark of resilience. Instead of shying away from failure, individuals view it as an indispensable companion on the road to delayed gratification. They understand that each failure brings them closer to their goals, refining their strategies and fortifying their resolve.

"Failure is not a period but a comma in the story of resilience, signaling that the best chapters are yet to be written."
– Anonymous

Embracing Failure as a Steppingstone:

- Failure as Feedback: Resilience thrives when failure is embraced as feedback. Instead of viewing failure as a verdict on one's abilities, resilient individuals see it as a valuable signal that guides refinement and improvement. Failure becomes a steppingstone rather than a stumbling block.

- **Iterative Progress:** The delayed gratification journey is marked by iterative progress. Each failure becomes an iteration, refining the approach, strategy, or skill set. Resilience is the engine that keeps individuals moving forward despite setbacks, constantly iterating toward their long-term goals.

- **Debunking the Instant Success Myth:** Resilience dispels the myth of instant success. It acknowledges that success is a process, often involving trial and error. Embracing failure is integral to this process, dispelling the illusion that success can be instantaneously achieved.

— 66 —

"If sure-footed, the greatest steppingstone is a failure."
– Allison A. Justo, Ed.D.

— 99 —

Allowing Criticism to Fuel Passion

Criticism, when embraced constructively, becomes a powerful catalyst for resilience. Rather than viewing criticism as a deterrent, individuals on the delayed gratification journey allow it to fuel their passion and commitment. Constructive criticism serves as a compass, guiding them toward improvement and refinement.

Criticism is reframed as valuable feedback, an external perspective that aids in self-reflection and personal development. Resilient individuals use criticism as a tool for honing their skills, adjusting their course, and staying true to their long-term vision. The ability to transform criticism into motivation demonstrates a profound level of resilience on the delayed gratification journey.

"Criticism, when embraced with resilience, becomes the wind that propels the sails of passion toward the horizon of enduring success."
– Anonymous

1. **Constructive Criticism as a Catalyst:** Resilience is fortified when individuals view criticism not as a deterrent but as a catalyst for improvement. Constructive criticism becomes a valuable resource for refining skills, strategies, and approaches on the delayed gratification journey.

2. **Separating Emotion from Feedback:** Resilient individuals develop the ability to separate the emotional impact of criticism from its constructive potential. Instead of being demoralized, they use criticism as a tool for self-assessment and growth.

3. **Passion as a Shield:** Resilience is intertwined with passion. When criticism is viewed as a reflection of one's commitment to a goal, it becomes easier to weather. Passion becomes a shield against discouragement, allowing individuals to stay focused on their long-term objectives.

Harnessing Resilience in the Delayed Gratification Journey:

1. **Mindful Reflection:** Resilience is cultivated through mindful reflection on setbacks. Taking the time to understand the emotional and practical aspects of challenges allows individuals to fortify their mental and emotional resilience.

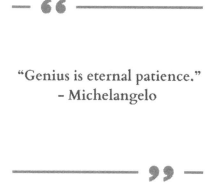

"Genius is eternal patience."
– Michelangelo

2. **Building a Support Network:** Resilience is not a solitary endeavor. Building a support network of mentors, peers, and advisors provides a valuable cushion during challenging times. Shared experiences and collective wisdom enhance the capacity to bounce back from setbacks.

3. **Continuous Adaptation:** Resilience thrives in an environment of continuous adaptation. The delayed gratification journey is dynamic, requiring individuals to adapt to changing circumstances, learn from failures, and refine their approach iteratively.

"It does not matter how slowly you go as long as you do not stop."
- Confucius

Novel Ideas in Building Resilience:

The Power of Reflection Journals: Keeping a reflection journal becomes a powerful tool for building resilience. This journal captures moments of setback, failure, or criticism and encourages individuals to reflect on their emotional responses, lessons learned, and strategies for improvement. This process aids in developing a proactive approach to resilience.

Resilience Affirmations: Incorporating resilience-affirming statements into daily routines reinforces a positive mindset. Affirmations such as "I embrace challenges as opportunities for growth" or "Every setback is a setup for a greater comeback" serve as constant reminders of the resilience mindset.

"Our greatest glory is not in never falling,
but in rising every time we fall."
- Confucius

Resilience Mentors: Seeking mentorship from individuals who have navigated similar challenges adds a dimension of shared wisdom and experience to the resilience journey. Learning from the stories of mentors provides insights into how setbacks can be transformative and integral to long-term success.

My wife (Allison), for example, had a wonderful professor who was her professional mentor while preparing her doctoral dissertation at Loyola University in Chicago. Since the first day I met Allison, she raved about how great her mentor was in helping stimulate her mind with creative juices as well as positively critiquing her writing and doctoral thesis. All of us can use similar supportive mentors who have a similarity of experience, skills, and wisdom.

Celebrating Micro-Resilience: Acknowledging and celebrating small victories, no matter how incremental, is a novel strategy for building resilience. Recognizing the ability to bounce back from minor setbacks reinforces the resilience mindset and contributes to the overall delayed gratification journey.

Conclusion: Resilience as the Silent Architect of Delayed Gratification

Resilience emerges as the silent architect, weaving through setbacks, obstacles, failures, and criticism to construct a narrative of enduring success. The resilience paradox teaches us that setbacks are not roadblocks but growth opportunities. Overcoming obstacles becomes a journey of self-discovery, and failure transforms into a teacher guiding us toward refinement. Criticism, when harnessed constructively, fuels the passion that propels us forward.

Building resilience is not just about enduring challenges but actively engaging with them, transforming adversity into a force that propels us toward our long-term goals. As individuals cultivate resilience on the delayed gratification journey, they not only fortify themselves against the storms of life but also emerge stronger, wiser, and more prepared to savor the delayed fruits of their labor.

Chapter 8

Celebrating Milestones – Small Wins, Big Victories

In the grand tapestry of delayed gratification, celebrating milestones is the thread that weaves motivation, progress, and commitment together. In the pursuit of delayed gratification and the realization of long-term goals, celebrating milestones along the way becomes a crucial aspect of the journey. This chapter emphasizes the significance of acknowledging not only the ultimate victories but also the small wins along the way. The importance of acknowledging and reveling in small victories, as well as the grand triumphs, is a critical part of the path to success. Engaging one's support structure—comprising mentors, family, friends, and coaches—adds depth to these celebrations, fostering a sense of shared achievement. Here, we explore the importance of recognizing and reveling in every step forward, making the journey towards delayed gratification a joyous and fulfilling one. We delve into the psychological and motivational benefits of these celebrations, emphasizing the role of one's support structure in amplifying the joy of achievement.

1. The Significance of Small Wins:

Small victories are the steppingstones to significant accomplishments. Small wins pave the way for monumental success.

Psychological Boost:

- **Positive Reinforcement:** Celebrating small wins provides a psychological boost. It reinforces the idea that efforts are bearing fruit, contributing to a positive mindset crucial for long-term success.

"Success is the sum of small efforts, repeated day in and day out."
- Robert Collier

- **Shifting Perspectives:** Celebrations contribute to a positive mindset. By focusing on achievements, individuals shift their perspective from challenges to opportunities, fostering resilience and determination.

"Great things are not done by impulse but by a
series of small things brought together."
- Vincent Van Gogh

Balancing Ambition with Contentment: Finding joy in
the journey, not just the destination.

Motivational Catalyst:

- **Fueling Momentum:** Small wins serve as a
catalyst for sustained motivation. They create a sense of
momentum, propelling individuals forward on their
journey of delayed gratification.

- **Inspiring the Journey:** Acknowledge and
celebrate small victories as they occur. Each step
forward, no matter how small, inspires motivation and
reinforces the commitment to the larger goal.

"It's the little details that are vital. Little things make big things happen."
– John Wooden

"What you get by achieving your goals is not as important as what you become by achieving your goals."
– Zig Ziglar

2. The Role of Support Structure:

Involving your support network enhances the joy of achievement.

Family and Friends:

• **Shared Joy:** Celebrating with family and friends amplifies the joy of achievement, fostering a collective sense of accomplishment and strengthening interpersonal bonds. My narrative revolves around the success of not only securing but also delivering a TEDx talk on "Delayed Gratification: Your Superpower to Success."

The talk has garnered significant attention, boasting nearly five million views (as of the current writing). The shared excitement within my family, particularly from my wife, has proven to be a potent motivator and a source of reinforcement, propelling me forward to the next milestone—another delivered TEDx talk titled "Unleashing the Drive Within: The OBSESSION Advantage to Unparalleled Success."

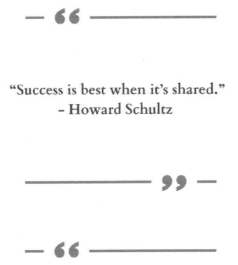

"Success is best when it's shared."
- Howard Schultz

"The strength of the family, like the strength of the army, is in its loyalty to each other."
- Mario Puzo

Mentors and Coaches:

- **Acknowledging Guidance:** Involving mentors and coaches in celebrations is a gesture of gratitude for their guidance. It also reaffirms the collaborative nature of the journey. Their guidance contributes significantly to the journey, and celebrating milestones together strengthens the mentor-mentee or coach-athlete relationship.

"A mentor is someone who allows you to
see the hope inside yourself."
- Oprah Winfrey

- **Fostering Camaraderie:** For those working within a team, shared celebrations foster camaraderie and teamwork. Acknowledging collective achievements reinforces the idea that success is a collaborative effort.

"Coming together is a beginning, staying together is progress, and working together is success."
- Henry Ford

3. Balancing Small Wins and Big Victories:

Celebrating both small and significant achievements is a holistic approach to success.

Setting Milestones:

- **Creating a Roadmap:** Set specific milestones along the path to a long-term goal. Celebrate each milestone as a marker of progress, contributing to the overall journey.

"Setting goals is the first step in turning the invisible into the visible."
- Tony Robbins

Acknowledging Effort:

- **Recognizing Hard Work:** Celebrate the effort invested, not just the outcome. Acknowledge the commitment and diligence put into the journey of delayed gratification.

"The only place where success comes before work is in the dictionary."
– Vidal Sassoon

- **Building Momentum:** Recognizing progress, irrespective of scale, builds momentum. Small victories are the steppingstones that collectively lead to significant achievements.

"It's not about how hard you hit. It's about how hard you can get hit and keep moving forward."
– Sylvester Stallone

4. The Power of Reflection:

Reflecting on achievements enhances the appreciation of the journey.

Gratitude Practice:

• **Counting Blessings:** Incorporate gratitude into celebrations. Reflect on the positive aspects of the journey, fostering a mindset of appreciation.

"Gratitude can transform common days into thanksgivings, turn routine jobs into joy, and change ordinary opportunities into blessings."
- William Arthur Ward

• **Balancing Ambition:** Express gratitude for the progress made. While ambition propels individuals forward, taking time to appreciate the journey ensures a healthy balance between ambition and contentment.

"Be thankful for what you have;
you'll end up having more. If you
concentrate on what you don't have,
you will never, ever have enough."
- Oprah Winfrey

- **Appreciating the Process:** Celebrate not only the destination but also the path taken. Finding joy in the journey transforms the pursuit of delayed gratification into a fulfilling and meaningful experience.

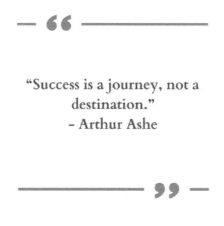

"Success is a journey, not a
destination."
- Arthur Ashe

Learning from Milestones:

- **Extracting Lessons:** Each milestone offers an opportunity to learn. Reflect on the strategies that led to success, adapting and refining them for future endeavors.

""

"Learn as if you will live forever, live like you will die tomorrow."
- Mahatma Gandhi

Conclusion

Celebrating milestones throughout the journey of delayed gratification is not merely a reward for accomplishments; it constitutes a vital aspect of the process. This crucial element serves to fortify commitment, amplify motivation, and enhance the joy inherent in the pursuit. Recognizing small victories, indulging in celebrations, involving one's support structure, and finding a balance between ambition and contentment make the journey more enriching.

As you navigate the path of delayed gratification, let each milestone stand as a testament to your progress and a source of inspiration for the steps yet to come. In the celebration of each victory, the symphony of your success resounds. Small wins fuel motivation, while significant victories mark substantial progress. The involvement of one's support structure further amplifies the joy of achievement. In the orchestration of success, each milestone becomes a melodious note contributing to the grand composition of enduring success. To echo the wisdom of Arthur Ashe, "The doing is often more important than the outcome."

Chapter 9

Building Your Tribe: The Power of Surrounding Yourself with Supportive People

In the intricate dance of delayed gratification, the company we keep plays a pivotal role. This chapter explores the profound impact of surrounding yourself with supportive individuals who understand the value of delayed gratification. From building a network of friends, mentors, and colleagues to the transformative power of guidance, motivation, and accountability, we'll navigate the nuances of curating a circle that enhances, rather than hinders, the delayed gratification journey. Moreover, we'll delve into the wisdom of taking advice from respected sources and the strategic art of selective sharing, safeguarding your vision and successes from the perils of envy and negative energy.

The Transformative Power of Guidance, Motivation, and Accountability:

1. **Common Values and Goals:** Building a network of supportive individuals begins with shared values and goals. Seek out those who understand and appreciate the principles of delayed gratification, as aligning with like-minded individuals fosters an environment conducive to long-term success.

2. **Diverse Perspectives:** Surrounding yourself with a diverse group brings varied perspectives, enriching your understanding of delayed gratification. Different experiences contribute to a robust support system, offering a tapestry of insights that can be applied to your unique journey.

3. **Mutual Respect:** Foster relationships based on mutual respect. The delayed gratification journey is deeply personal, and having individuals who respect your values and decisions creates a foundation for a supportive community.

4. **Cultivating Supportive Friendships:** Delayed gratification is often a lonely road, and having friends who understand its value is invaluable. Cultivate relationships with individuals who share similar values and aspirations. These friends become pillars of support during challenging times.

"Surround yourself with only people
who are going to lift you higher."
- Oprah Winfrey

5. **Mentors as Guiding Lights:** Seek out mentors who have walked the path of delayed gratification. Their guidance, based on experience, becomes a beacon of wisdom. A mentor can provide insights, share lessons from their journey, and offer a roadmap to navigate challenges.

"The delicate balance of mentoring
someone is not creating them in your
own image but giving them the
opportunity to create themselves."
- Steven Spielberg

Mentors, individuals who have traversed similar paths, offer invaluable guidance. Their wisdom becomes a compass, providing direction and insights that can save time and energy on the delayed gratification journey.

"A mentor is someone who sees more
talent and ability within you than you see
in yourself and helps bring it out of you."
- Bob Proctor

6. **Motivation from Peers:** Peers who share your commitment to delayed gratification become a wellspring of motivation. The shared journey creates a sense of camaraderie, inspiring each other to persist through challenges and celebrate successes, no matter how small.

"You become like the five people you
spend the most time with."
- Jim Rohn

7. **Colleagues as Accountability Partners:** In professional spheres, colleagues can play a pivotal role as accountability partners. A supportive work environment fosters collaboration, encourages each

other's growth, and contributes to a collective success mindset. Having accountability partners is akin to having a built-in support system. They help maintain focus, ensuring that commitments to long-term goals are upheld. Accountability partners create a structure that reinforces delayed gratification principles.

"Great things in business are never done by one person. They're done by a team of people."
– Steve Jobs

The Role of Supportive People:

Guidance in the Maze of Decisions: Supportive individuals offer guidance in navigating the intricate maze of decisions. Their varied perspectives and experiences enrich your decision-making process, ensuring that choices align with the principles of delayed gratification. In my case, my most supportive friend and mentor is my wife, whose brilliant ideas I respect and whom I know will never mislead me and always have my best recommendations in mind. This is not always the case for spouses to be so supportive as I am also aware of spouses who envy the successes of each other and view it as a competition between themselves.

Motivation in Moments of Doubt: The journey of delayed gratification is rife with moments of doubt. Supportive people act as motivators, reminding you of the long-term goals, instilling confidence, and fueling the perseverance needed to stay on course.

Accountability for Consistent Progress: Supportive individuals hold you accountable for your actions. Whether friends, mentors, or colleagues, they become checkpoints in your journey, ensuring that you stay true to your commitments and consistently progress toward your goals.

"A real friend is one who walks in
when the rest of the world walks out."
- Walter Winchell

Taking Advice Selectively:

1. **Respecting the Source of Advice:** In the realm of delayed gratification, the quality of advice is crucial. Take advice only from those you respect and admire.

Consider the source's experience, values, and track record before incorporating advice into your decision-making process.

"Don't take advice from someone you
wouldn't trade places with."
– Darren Hardy

2. **Aligning Advice with Values:** Ensure that the advice aligns with your values and the principles of delayed gratification. Well-intentioned advice may not always apply to your unique journey, and discernment is key in selecting guidance that resonates with your path. By being selective in the advice you follow, you ensure that your actions remain congruent with the principles of delayed gratification.

"Your time is limited, don't waste it
living someone else's life."
- Steve Jobs

3. **Balancing Multiple Perspectives:** Delayed gratification often involves weighing multiple perspectives. Seek advice from a diverse range of sources, ensuring that your decisions are well-informed and consider different angles. This multifaceted approach enhances the richness of your decision-making process.

"It is the long history of humankind that those who learned to collaborate and improvise most effectively have prevailed."
- Charles Darwin

4. **Quality over Quantity:** In a world flooded with information, the art of discernment becomes crucial. Take advice only from sources you genuinely respect and

admire. It's not about the quantity of advice but the quality that aligns with your values and goals.

5. **Expertise and Experience:** Seek advice from individuals with relevant expertise and experience. Their insights carry the weight of practical knowledge, offering guidance tailored to the nuances of the delayed gratification journey.

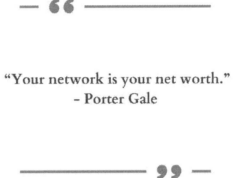

"Your network is your net worth."
– Porter Gale

The Strategic Art of Selective Sharing:

1. **Protecting Your Vision:** Delayed gratification often involves pursuing unconventional paths. Not everyone may understand or support your vision. Selective sharing safeguards your dreams from those who might cast doubt or negativity on your journey. While sharing your vision and successes is integral for personal affirmation, it's crucial to do so strategically. Not everyone in your circle may genuinely celebrate your journey. Strategic sharing involves selecting individuals who genuinely support your aspirations.

"Don't tell people your dreams. Show them."
– Unknown

"Don't share too much of your private
information too soon, or else someone else
may steal your idea."
– Rebeca M. Justo

2. **Mitigating Envy:** Envy can be a silent saboteur. By sharing your successes selectively, you mitigate the risk of attracting negative energy. Surrounding yourself with supportive individuals who genuinely celebrate your victories shields your journey from envy's corrosive effects. Guard against sharing your vision with individuals prone to envy or those who may not understand the delayed gratification mindset. Be discerning in choosing confidants who will genuinely celebrate your successes.

3. **Preserving Positive Energy:** Your vision is a precious commodity. Sharing it with those who uplift rather than undermine preserves positive energy. Build a circle where your successes are met with encouragement, fostering an environment conducive to delayed gratification. Negative energy can hinder your journey. Not everyone needs to know every detail of your vision. Protect your dreams from unnecessary negativity by choosing when and with whom to share your successes.

Conclusion

In the intricate tapestry of delayed gratification, the individuals we choose to surround ourselves with can either propel us forward or act as anchors. Building a tribe of supportive friends, mentors, family, and colleagues who truly comprehend the journey is indispensable. Their guidance, motivation, and accountability serve as catalysts for success. The art of selective sharing, coupled with discerning advice, ensures that your delayed gratification journey remains aligned with your vision, shielded from the perils of negativity and envy.

As you curate your circle, bear in mind that in the symphony of delayed gratification, the harmonious notes are often struck by those who genuinely understand and support your pursuit of enduring success. Surrounding yourself with supportive people is not just a luxury but a strategic choice in the delayed gratification journey. Friends, mentors, and colleagues become essential pillars of guidance, motivation, and accountability. The art of selectively taking advice ensures that the counsel received aligns with your values, and strategic sharing protects your vision from potential pitfalls. As you build your network of support, remember that the delayed gratification journey is not a solo endeavor, and the right support can transform challenges into triumphs on the road to enduring success.

Chapter 10

The Art of Choosing a Life Partner: Delayed Gratification in Matters of the Heart

In the grand orchestration of life, selecting a life partner is a crucial movement that echoes through the years, influencing the melody of one's journey. Perhaps no decision is as pivotal, intricate, and impactful as the choice of a life partner. This chapter explores the delicate dance between the heart and the mind, navigating the seas of emotions and rationality, all while adhering to the principles of delayed gratification. From the initial spark to the enduring flame, the journey of selecting a life partner is a nuanced exploration of shared values, goals, and a commitment to building a future together.

- **Navigating the Sea of Relationships: Beyond Superficial Tides** *Hormones and Physical Appearance:* The journey begins with the acknowledgment of the potent allure of physical attraction and the rush of hormones. However, it's crucial not to let these transient highs dictate the course of a lifelong commitment. In a world often driven by instant gratification, it's easy to succumb to the allure of physical attraction and immediate chemistry. However, building a life together requires a deeper foundation. The delayed gratification approach urges individuals to look beyond the surface, focusing on shared cultural, social, and intellectual values. Similar life goals become the cornerstone upon which a lasting connection can be built.

"The most beautiful things in life are not things. They're people, places, memories, and pictures. They're feelings and moments and smiles and laughter."
– Unknown

> "Love at first sight is easy to understand; it's when two people have been looking at each other for a lifetime that it becomes a miracle."
> – Amy Bloom

- **Similarities vs. Differences:**

Cultural, Social, and Intellectual Alignment: The foundation of a strong partnership lies in shared values, cultural background, and intellectual pursuits. It's a melody composed of common interests and goals that resonate through the years. The age-old adage of "opposites attract" is often challenged when it comes to the long-term viability of a relationship. While differences can add spice to life, a solid partnership requires a significant degree of common ground. It's essential to recognize that enduring partnerships often thrive on shared interests and life goals.

This chapter explores the delicate balance between shared interests and complementary traits, emphasizing the importance of finding a middle ground that fosters harmony. Please understand that this chapter speaks in terms of generalities and recommendations that, in my opinion, are statistically relevant. This implies that indeed there are exceptions to my recommendations in which individuals from different cultures, ethnicities, and with different values can certainly become one and sustain a life-long joyful partnership. However, this is the exception rather than the rule.

"It is not a lack of love, but a lack of friendship that makes unhappy marriages."
– Friedrich Nietzsche

• The Role of Time and Patience

Knowing Your Preferences: The path to a successful long-term commitment involves a period of exploration and experimentation. Dating various individuals helps in understanding personal preferences, strengths, and areas of compatibility. The rush to commitment, fueled by societal expectations or personal timelines, can lead to hasty decisions. The delayed gratification perspective encourages individuals to take their time, allowing relationships to unfold naturally. Experimenting with various personalities, dating different people, and understanding one's preferences become crucial steps in the process.

"The best thing to hold onto in life is each other."
– Audrey Hepburn

"The best way to find out if you can trust somebody is to trust them."
– Ernest Hemingway

- **Extricating Yourself for Future Growth**

Overcoming Instant Gratification: Delaying the commitment to marriage until one has overcome the allure of instant gratification is a crucial step. It allows individuals to mature emotionally, ensuring that the decision is driven by a deeper understanding of oneself and the partner. Recognizing the signs of a relationship that may not withstand the test of time requires courage and self-awareness. Delayed gratification prompts individuals to prioritize their long-term happiness over short-term pleasures. Extricating oneself from a relationship that doesn't align with one's vision for the future is an act of self-love and an investment in personal growth. Recognizing when a relationship isn't aligned with long-term goals requires the courage to put oneself first. Extricating oneself sooner rather than later is an act of self-preservation.

— 66 ———————

"Sometimes good things fall apart so
better things can fall together."
– Marilyn Monroe

——————— 99 —

- **The Journey to Financial and Emotional Security:**

Once the right life partner is found, the journey of delayed gratification extends into building a shared future. Financial security, the choice of a home, and the decision to start a family are all significant milestones that demand patience and thoughtful planning. Achieving financial security as a couple precedes expanding the family. It's a deliberate process of ensuring stability before taking on the responsibilities of parenthood. This chapter explores the delicate balance between achieving personal goals and building a life together.

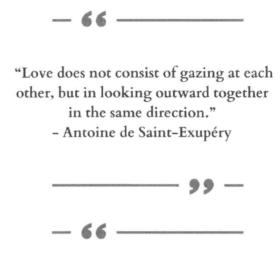

"Love does not consist of gazing at each other, but in looking outward together in the same direction."
– Antoine de Saint-Exupéry

"Marriage is not just spiritual communion; it is also remembering to take out the trash."
– Joyce Brothers

- **The Continuing Saga of Delayed Gratification:**

Selecting a life partner marks the commencement of a lifelong journey, one that requires a commitment to delayed gratification at every turn. The commitment to a life partner evolves into the commitment to building a family. Delayed gratification extends to the careful consideration of timing, finances, and the emotional readiness for the complexities of family life. As couples navigate the complexities of marriage, family, and shared dreams, the principles of patience, compromise, and a shared vision become the guiding stars.

"A successful marriage requires falling in love many times, always with the same person."
- Mignon McLaughlin

"Family is not an important thing. It's everything."
- Michael J. Fox

In my life's journey, it was imperative for me to delay starting a family until I married "late" and began having children at the age of forty-three. Now, I am blessed to have been married to the love of my life for over twenty years with three teenage children. I certainly would not preach to anyone to necessarily wait until my age to start a family, but the basic point is that there are significant advantages to waiting (e.g. financial and emotional security), whereas there are other advantages to starting a bit sooner such as around the age of thirty or so (e.g. more adventuresome with greater energy and hopefully being able to enjoy future grandchildren for a longer period).

Conclusion

Delayed gratification manifests in the patient search for the right person, the careful consideration of compatibility, and the intentional delay of major commitments until a solid foundation is laid. In matters of the heart, the art of choosing a life partner is a testament to the principles of delayed gratification. From the initial stages of attraction to the shared milestones of building a life together, the journey is intricate, challenging, and deeply rewarding. As individuals navigate the complexities of relationships, the wisdom of delaying immediate desires for the promise of a richer, more fulfilling future emerges as the cornerstone of lasting love.

Chapter 11

Mastering the Art of Wise Saving and Prudent Investing

In the journey of delayed gratification, mastering the art of saving and investing wisely is a fundamental step towards building a secure and stable financial future. This chapter explores the recommended steps for responsible money management, the conservative approach to saving and investing, and the cultivation of habits that make financial prudence a natural part of daily life. We delve into the distinction between needs and wants, delaying spending on non-essential items, and the crucial task of building financial stability for the future.

The Foundation: Wise Saving

Set Clear Financial Goals: Begin by setting clear and achievable financial goals. Whether it's an emergency fund, a down payment on a house, or retirement savings, having well-defined objectives provides a roadmap for your financial journey. Taking control of your finances is the first step towards delayed gratification.

"A budget is telling your money where to go instead of wondering where it went."
– Dave Ramsey

Create a Realistic Budget: Develop a detailed budget that aligns with your goals. Categorize expenses into needs and wants and allocate a portion of your income towards savings and investments. A realistic budget forms the backbone of disciplined financial management. Develop a budget that aligns with your income and expenses. Be realistic about your spending habits and prioritize essential expenses.

> "The stock market is a device for transferring money from the impatient to the patient."
> – Warren Buffett

Automate Your Savings: Make saving a habit by automating the process. Set up automatic transfers to your savings or investment accounts each month. Automation removes the need for constant decision-making, making saving a consistent part of your financial routine. This habit ensures that saving becomes a recurring, effortless task.

> "Don't save what is left after spending; spend what is left after saving."
> – Warren Buffett

> "The habit of saving is itself an education; it fosters every virtue, teaches self-denial, cultivates the sense of order, trains to forethought, and so broadens the mind."
> – T.T. Munger

Emergency Fund: Prioritize building an emergency fund. Establish an emergency fund to cover unexpected expenses. Having this financial buffer provides peace of mind and prevents the need to dip into long-term savings. Having a financial safety net ensures that unexpected expenses don't derail your overall financial plan. Aim for three to six months' worth of living expenses in your emergency fund.

> "The goal isn't more money. The goal is living life on your terms."
> – Chris Brogan

"An emergency fund is like insurance
for peace of mind."
– Suze Orman

The Art of Prudent Investing:

Conservative strategies ensure steady growth without unnecessary risk.

Educate Yourself: Before diving into the world of investing, invest time in educating yourself. Understand the basics of different investment vehicles, risk management, and the power of compound interest. Informed decisions are the bedrock of successful investing.

"Successful investing is about managing
risk, not avoiding it."
– Benjamin Graham

"The four most dangerous words in
investing are: 'This time it's different."
- Sir John Templeton

Avoid putting all your eggs in one basket. Diversify your investment portfolio across different asset classes to spread risk. A diversified approach helps mitigate the impact of volatility in any single investment.

"Diversification is protection against
ignorance. It makes little sense if you
know what you are doing."
- Warren Buffett

Long-Term Perspective: Adopt a long-term perspective when it comes to investing. The power of compounding works most effectively over extended periods. Patiently staying the course during market fluctuations is often the key to substantial returns. Avoid the temptation to chase short-term gains and focus on the gradual growth of your investments.

"The best investment you can make is
in yourself."
- Warren Buffett

Risk Tolerance: Assess your risk tolerance and tailor your investment strategy accordingly. Understand that all investments carry some level of risk and align your choices with your ability to weather market fluctuations.

"Risk comes from not knowing what
you're doing."
- Warren Buffett

Creating Habits for Financial Success:

Transform financial prudence into a habit that requires minimal effort.

Consistency is Key: Cultivate the habit of consistency in saving and investing. Small, regular contributions can accumulate significantly over time. Consistency also helps in weathering market volatility.

"It's not how much money you make, but how much money you keep, how hard it works for you, and how many generations you keep it for."
– Robert Kiyosaki

Automate Investments: Similar to automating savings, automate your investments. Set up regular contributions to your investment accounts. Automation eliminates the need for constant decision-making and emotional reactions to market fluctuations. As I preach to my nineteen-year-old son who works part-time during college school breaks, automate your paycheck such that a minimum of ten to twenty percent of your gross pay automatically gets deposited into a high-interest savings account (which I recommend looking at no more than monthly) or an index fund (for more advanced investors), whereas the remainder of the paycheck is deposited into your regular debit or checking account. In reality, if our son were a bit more of a planner, I would suggest a substantially higher savings rate considering that most of his day-to-day expenditures are paid for by me, other than going out with friends to dinner, movies or a concert.

"The stock market is filled with individuals who know the price of everything, but the value of nothing."
– Philip Fisher

Regularly Review and Adjust: Periodically review your financial goals, budget, and investment strategy. Life circumstances change, and your financial plan should evolve accordingly. Regular reviews help in staying on track and making necessary adjustments.

*"The goal of a successful trader is to make
the best trades. Money is secondary."*
– Alexander Elder

Delaying Non-Essential Spending:

Conscious Consumption: Cultivate mindfulness in your spending habits. Before making a purchase, ask yourself whether it aligns with your long-term goals or if it's a momentary want.

Distinguishing Wants vs. Needs: Differentiate between wants and needs. Prioritize spending on needs and delay gratification for wants. Understanding this distinction is crucial in maintaining financial discipline. Again, using the example of our oldest son, he chooses to spend his extra money (e.g. from birthday or Christmas gifts) to buy concert tickets or take his girlfriend out to a fancy dinner, rather than saving for his future "needs."

Delayed Gratification for Long-Term Gain:
Embrace the concept of delayed gratification when it
comes to non-essential spending. By delaying immediate
desires, you free up resources for more significant, long-
term financial goals. Delay spending on non-essential
items to build discipline. Allow time for thoughtful
consideration, and often, the initial desire diminishes.

> "Success is not the key to happiness.
> Happiness is the key to success. If you love
> what you are doing, you will be successful."
> - Albert Schweitzer

Debt Management:

Prioritize Debt Repayment: Focus on paying off high-interest debts to free up resources for savings and investments. Managing debt is integral to building financial stability. The most important advice I would give to anyone, whether it is our children or the reader of this book, is do your best to AVOID debt (other than your primary residence or maybe "frugal debt" with a necessary automobile and low monthly payments with low interest). Avoid credit card debt at all costs, to make sure you pay off your credit card(s) monthly and not accumulate the very high interest associated with credit card debt. Whenever possible, try to purchase using cash or debit, instead of credit, if for any reason you feel you are not disciplined enough to manage your credit card spending. In this case, only use your credit cards for true emergencies assuming you do not have an emergency fund set aside. In reality, if you have an emergency fund, then either cut up your credit cards or leave them in a safe, secure place at home but do not carry them in your wallet to avoid the temptation to use them.

"The best way to predict your future is to create it."
– Peter Drucker

Insurance Coverage:

Protecting Assets: Ensure adequate insurance coverage for health, property, and life. Additionally, as I explained in an earlier chapter regarding my own example with my mother, I feel that consideration of long-term care insurance for oneself, a spouse, or a loved one who may need support in their aging years, is something to consider purchasing early in life while one is still insurable. Protecting against unforeseen circumstances safeguards your financial stability.

—— 66 ——————

"Insurance is a way to plan for the unexpected.
Life insurance is about protecting the ones
you love."
– Dave Ramsey

—————————— 99 —

Building Financial Stability:

Strengthening your financial foundation ensures a secure future.

Savings for Financial Stability: Savings form the foundation of financial stability. Having a robust savings plan provides a buffer against unexpected expenses, job loss, or economic downturns. As I discussed earlier, I would recommend setting a goal of automating one's savings for a minimum of twenty percent of one's gross pay each paycheck. Once you start doing this for a few payroll cycles, you will quickly realize that you will no longer even be aware of the lesser pay going into your checking account. Some will also advocate automating some of their gross pay going into a separate account for charitable purposes...many recommend five to ten percent of gross pay, although this will be a personal decision and choice for each individual.

"Save money and money will save you."
- Jamaican Proverb

Investing for Future Security: Investing wisely is a strategy for future security. A well-managed investment portfolio can provide financial stability in retirement or during unforeseen circumstances.

"Investing should be more like watching paint dry or watching grass grow. If you want excitement, take $800 and go to Las Vegas."
- Paul Samuelson

Continuous Learning: Stay committed to continuous learning about personal finance and investment strategies. Financial literacy empowers you to make informed decisions, enhancing your ability to build and maintain financial stability. Commit to ongoing financial education. Understanding the nuances of personal finance empowers you to make informed decisions for long-term success.

"It is what we know already that often prevents us from learning."
- Claude Bernard

"The more you learn, the more you earn."
- Warren Buffett

Conclusion

Saving and investing wisely is not just about accumulating wealth; it's a journey that requires discipline, patience, and a strategic mindset. Responsible money management, conservative saving and investing, and the cultivation of habits that make financial prudence second nature are the cornerstones of wealth-building. Distinguishing between needs and wants, delaying spending on non-essential items, and building financial stability contribute to a robust foundation for enduring success. In the symphony of delayed gratification, the chapter on saving and investing wisely plays a melodious tune that resonates through the halls of financial prosperity.

Mastering the art of wise saving and prudent investing is a transformative step in the delayed gratification journey. By setting clear goals, creating consistent habits, and distinguishing between needs and wants, you lay the groundwork for financial stability and long-term success. Famous quotes from financial luminaries serve as guiding principles, emphasizing the timeless wisdom of disciplined financial management. Remember, the key lies not just in accumulating wealth but in using it judiciously to fulfill your life's aspirations and contribute positively to the world.

Chapter 12

Navigating the Labyrinth of Vices – Delaying the Instant Fix

In the grand scheme of life, vices often present themselves as alluring shortcuts to instant gratification. This chapter delves into the various vices that promise immediate highs but ultimately hinder the pursuit of long-term success. Each vice is dissected, offering alternative methods that embrace delayed gratification, accompanied by the wisdom of unique quotes from influential figures.

1. Drug Addiction: Escaping the Instant High

The Allure of Immediate Escape:

- **Instant Gratification vs. Natural Highs:** The instant high from drugs offers a fleeting escape. Choosing instead to pursue natural highs through achievements, such as academic success or personal accomplishments, allows for a more enduring sense of fulfillment. Drugs offer a swift escape from reality, providing instant gratification. However, the consequences of this momentary pleasure can be devastating in the long run.

"Drugs take you to hell, disguised as heaven."
- Donald Lyn Frost

Delayed Gratification Alternative:

- **Achievement through Effort:** Instead of seeking a quick fix, channeling energy into academic achievements, hard work, and personal growth can provide a more enduring sense of accomplishment.

"Success is not an accident. It's the result of hard work, learning, sacrifice, and most of all, love of what you are doing."
– Pele

2. Alcohol — In Moderation: Navigating the Social Libation

Instant Elixir of Confidence:

- **Temporary Boost:** Alcohol can offer a temporary boost in self-esteem and confidence. However, moderation is key, as excessive consumption leads to diminishing returns. Opting for moderation and finding self-worth through genuine achievements fosters a more stable and lasting sense of confidence.

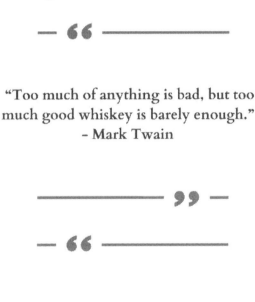

"Too much of anything is bad, but too much good whiskey is barely enough."
- Mark Twain

"Moderation in all things, especially moderation."
- Ralph Waldo Emerson

Delayed Gratification Alternative:

- **Building Confidence through Achievements:** Instead of relying on alcohol for confidence, achieving personal and academic milestones can instill a lasting sense of self-esteem and self-worth.

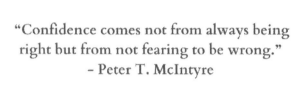

"Confidence comes not from always being right but from not fearing to be wrong."
– Peter T. McIntyre

3. Social Media: Navigating the Infinite Scroll

Instant Validation:

- **Comparison Culture:** Social media platforms offer a constant stream of images portraying success, wealth, and fame, fostering a culture of instant validation.

"Comparison is the thief of joy."
- Theodore Roosevelt

Delayed Gratification Alternative:

- **Strategic Engagement:** Using social media for business-related purposes, inspiration, and limited personal use allows for a healthier relationship with these platforms. Balancing its use for business and inspiration, in moderation, can transform it into a tool for positive growth rather than a source of envy.

"Social media is about sociology and psychology more than technology."
- Brian Solis

"Social media is not about the exploitation of
technology but service to community."
- Simon Mainwaring

- **Unlimited Scrolling vs. Purposeful Engagement:** The never-ending scroll of platforms like TikTok, Instagram and Reels can become a mindless escape. Redirecting that time towards purposeful engagement fosters meaningful connections and personal growth.

"Quality over quantity. Always."
– Unknown

4. Gambling/Sports Betting: Temptation of Quick Gains

Adrenaline Rush of Quick Wins:

- **Instant Thrill:** The allure of quick financial gains through gambling and sports betting is a tempting proposition, driven by the thrill of instantaneous wins. Advertisements often glamorize the allure of quick wins through gambling. Embracing patience and delayed gratification shifts the focus to more sustainable forms of success.

"The only way to see a positive outcome in your life is to put positive action into it."
- Wesam Fawzi

Delayed Gratification Alternative:

- **Investing in Knowledge and Skills:** Rather than relying on chance, investing time in acquiring knowledge and skills can lead to more sustainable success.

"Patience is the key to contentment."
– Muhammad Iqbal

5. Get Rich Quick Schemes: Navigating Illusions of Wealth

The Illusion of Swift Prosperity Attracting the Young and Impatient:

• **Empty Promises:** Schemes promising quick riches, especially in the online realm, often appeal to the desire for instant success. Get-rich-quick schemes appeal to impatience. Redirecting that energy towards building genuine wealth over time through hard work and perseverance yields more meaningful results.

"Wealth is the ability to fully experience life."
– Henry David Thoreau

Delayed Gratification Alternative:

- **Building a Sustainable Business:** Instead of falling for illusions, building a sustainable business requires patience, effort, and a commitment to long-term success.

"Success usually comes to those who are too busy to be looking for it."
– Henry David Thoreau

6. Pornography: Escaping the Instant Pleasure and Cultivating Genuine Connections

Instant Gratification of Desires:

- **Immediate Pleasure:** Pornography offers a quick fix for desires, providing immediate pleasure but lacking the depth and intimacy of true connection. Opting for genuine connections and building real relationships allows for a deeper and more fulfilling sense of intimacy.

"Sexuality is a window into the soul, but
pornography is a door."
- Gail Dines

Delayed Gratification Alternative:

- **Building Genuine Connections:** Cultivating real relationships and connections, based on shared values and mutual respect, leads to a more fulfilling and lasting form of gratification.

"Intimacy is not purely physical. It's the act of
connecting with someone so deeply, you feel
like you can see into their soul."
- Unknown

Conclusion: The Triumph of Patience

In the intricate dance between vices and delayed gratification, success hinges on recognizing the illusions of instant pleasure and opting for the path of enduring triumph. Navigating the tempting allure of drugs, alcohol, social media, gambling, get-rich-quick schemes, and pornography requires individuals to embrace patience and make a conscious effort toward long-term achievements. This commitment becomes the antidote to fleeting highs.

In the labyrinth of vices promising instant gratification, the road less traveled is that of delayed gratification. As individuals redirect their energies towards accomplishments, moderation, purposeful engagement, patience, genuine wealth, and authentic connections, the rewards not only endure but also undergo a transformative shift. The liberation from vices signifies the triumph of delayed gratification, a testament to the resilience of the human spirit over the allure of instant satisfaction.

Chapter 13

The Mental Health Pitfalls of Instant Gratification: A Deeper Dive

Instant gratification, the desire for immediate pleasure or reward without delay, has become increasingly prevalent in modern society, fueled by technology, social media, and consumer culture. While this phenomenon has been extensively discussed in the context of personal life, its impact in the professional realm is equally noteworthy. Business leaders need to comprehend the potential ramifications of instant gratification on their organizations.

Instant gratification spills into interpersonal relationships, both personal and professional. In the workplace, employees may expect immediate responses or attention from colleagues and superiors. This can result in unrealistic expectations, potentially leading to disappointment and strained relationships.

The perpetual pursuit of instant gratification can take a toll on mental health. Stress, anxiety, and depression may escalate when individuals face obstacles that require time and effort to overcome. The expectation of immediate results can lead to feelings of hopelessness if outcomes are not swift, impacting overall well-being.

Individuals with a strong desire for immediate gratification are more prone to stress and negative emotions. On the contrary, those capable of delaying gratification tend to experience positive emotions and achieve long-term success.

The desire for instant gratification impacts relationships and emphasizes the frustration and disillusionment that can arise when immediate responses or attention are not received.

The impact of instant gratification on mental health, specifically within the realm of social media, emphasizes the pressure to be constantly connected and responsive, contributing to anxiety, FOMO, and potential addiction. The fear of missing out (FOMO) is an emotional response to the belief that other people are living better, more satisfying lives, or that important opportunities are being missed. FOMO often leads to feelings of unease, dissatisfaction, depression, and stress.

The apparent conflict between living in the moment and delaying gratification can create internal turmoil. However, both aspects can be valuable tools for a fulfilling life. Living in the moment allows the full experience of life's joys while delaying gratification sets the stage for future success and happiness.

One family example is our eldest son who loves living in the moment and is one of the most sociable human beings I have ever seen as he befriends strangers on vacations and away at college. While he enjoys the daily pleasures, he is also one of the hardest working teens I have seen as he spends as much time as possible working part-time while on vacation at home so he can save money for his future. This is a nice blend of instant as well as delayed gratification.

As teenagers, the brain stops growing in size by early adolescence. However, the brain continues to develop and mature well into the mid-to-late 20s. The pre-frontal cortex is the last part of the brain to mature and is responsible for good decision-making, planning, and ultimately choosing delayed gratification vs instant gratification.

The key lies in striking a balance between these seemingly opposing forces. By embracing the present while making sacrifices for the future, individuals can savor immediate pleasures and build a foundation for enduring success. It's not an either-or scenario but a harmonious integration of both approaches that leads to a rich and rewarding life.

Let's take a deeper dive into unveiling the power of delayed gratification:

The Stanford Marshmallow Experiment, conducted in the late 1960s by psychologist Walter Mischel and his colleagues, stands as a landmark study in understanding the role of delayed gratification in human behavior, particularly in children. The experiment aimed to explore the cognitive and emotional processes involved in the ability to resist immediate rewards for the promise of a greater reward in the future.

The setup was relatively simple. A child, typically around the age of four to six years of age, sat in a room with a marshmallow (or another tempting treat) placed in front of them. The researcher presented a choice: the child could either eat the marshmallow immediately or wait for the researcher to return in about fifteen minutes, at which point they would be rewarded with an additional marshmallow.

The initial observations were straightforward. Some children succumbed to the temptation, consuming the marshmallow almost immediately. Others, however, demonstrated remarkable self-discipline, resisting the immediate pleasure for the promise of a greater reward later.

The true significance of the Stanford Marshmallow Experiment emerged when researchers tracked the participants longitudinally over the years. The ability to delay gratification demonstrated in those early years proved to have profound implications for the individuals' later lives.

1. **Academic Success:** The children who exhibited patience and resisted the immediate temptation tended to perform better academically. They scored higher on standardized tests and displayed a greater ability to concentrate in school.

2. **Emotional Regulation:** Delayed gratification was linked to improved emotional regulation. Participants showed a better capacity to handle stress and frustration, leading to fewer behavioral problems.

3. **Social Competence:** Individuals who mastered the art of waiting for a greater reward demonstrated enhanced social competence. They were more adept at forming and maintaining relationships and exhibiting better interpersonal skills.

4. **Health and Addictions:** Perhaps most strikingly, the ability to delay gratification was associated with better health outcomes. Individuals who could resist immediate temptations were less likely to struggle with addiction issues later in life.

One of the key takeaways from the Stanford Marshmallow Experiment is that the capacity for delayed gratification is not fixed; it can be taught and cultivated. Mischel and his team observed that the strategies employed by the children who succeeded in delaying gratification were diverse. Some covered their eyes, while others sang or played to distract themselves. These self-distraction techniques indicated a crucial aspect of the skill — the ability to redirect attention away from the tempting reward.

The Marshmallow Experiment transcends its original scope and carries implications for various aspects of human life. It underscores the significance of self-discipline and the role it plays in shaping our futures. The findings suggest that the skills learned in childhood, particularly the ability to delay gratification, are not only predictors of academic success but also influential in determining the overall trajectory of one's life.

The Stanford Marshmallow Experiment remains an enduring symbol of the importance of delayed gratification in human development. It not only showcased the psychological complexity behind seemingly simple choices but also provided insights that reverberate across the fields of education, psychology, and behavioral economics. The capacity to delay gratification, a skill honed in the early years of life, emerges as a guiding force that shapes academic achievements, emotional well-being, and overall life success.

While instant gratification might offer momentary pleasure, its pervasive influence on mental health, relationships, and workplace dynamics necessitates a nuanced understanding. Striking a balance between immediate rewards and delayed gratification is crucial for individual well-being as well as business success.

Investing in education on this matter becomes imperative for individuals and organizations. Furthermore, implementing principles and processes that support a proper balance can help mitigate the negative effects of instant gratification. By fostering a culture that values both short-term wins and long-term goals, both our personal as well as our professional lives can navigate the complex landscape of desires and achievements.

"Strength does not come from the body. It
comes from the will."
– Arnold Schwarzenegger

"Success is the result of perfection, hard work,
learning from failure, loyalty, and persistence."
– Colin Powell

"Delayed gratification is a powerful tool for
success. If you can make yourself wait, you
can achieve anything."
– Unknown

Chapter 14

The Cuban Triad for Unparalleled Success

In the narrative of my journey as a Cuban refugee coming to the United States at the age of three, the chapters of self-discipline, perseverance/resilience, and delayed gratification form an unparalleled triad for achieving success. This chapter delves into the intricate details of each element, examining how they intersect, interplay, and harmonize to shape not only my narrative but also serve as a universal blueprint for achievement.

1. Self-Discipline: The Keystone of Achievement

a) Definition and Essence of Self-Discipline:

• **Self-Mastery:** Self-discipline is the cornerstone of success, representing the mastery of one's impulses and desires. It's the conscious choice to master oneself, resisting immediate gratification for the sake of long-term goals and aligning actions with purpose.

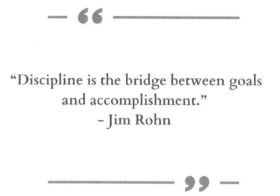

"Discipline is the bridge between goals and accomplishment."
– Jim Rohn

b) Personal Journey with Self-Discipline:

• **Navigating Challenges:** As a Cuban refugee, self-discipline became my guiding force. The challenges of adapting to a new country and culture required a disciplined approach to learning, assimilating, and striving for success.

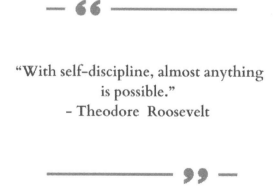

"With self–discipline, almost anything is possible."
– Theodore Roosevelt

c) Implementing Self-Discipline:

• **Habits and Consistency:** The implementation of self-discipline involves cultivating positive habits and maintaining consistency. It's the commitment to daily actions that align with overarching goals.

"We are what we repeatedly do. Excellence, then, is not an act but a habit."
– Aristotle

2. Perseverance/Resilience: Triumph Over Adversity

a) Defining Perseverance and Resilience:

• **The Shield Against Adversity:** The armor that transforms challenges into stepping stones.

• **Adaptability:** Perseverance is the ability to navigate through adversity with adaptability, recognizing that setbacks are not roadblocks but growth opportunities.

> "It's not that I'm so smart, it's just that I
> stay with problems longer."
> - Albert Einstein

- **Endurance in the Face of Challenges:** Perseverance and resilience encapsulate the ability to endure setbacks, bounce back from adversity, and emerge stronger from challenges.

> "The human capacity for burden is like bamboo—far more flexible than you'd ever believe at first glance."
> - Jodi Picoult

b) Personal Triumphs of Perseverance:

- **Overcoming Setbacks:** My journey as a Cuban refugee embodies the spirit of perseverance. From the challenges of starting anew in the United States to facing cultural and linguistic barriers, resilience became a guiding force.

"In three words I can sum up everything
I've learned about life: it goes on."
– Robert Frost

c) **Cultivating Perseverance:**

• **Mindset and Adaptability:** Perseverance is cultivated through a resilient mindset and adaptability. It's the ability to view challenges as opportunities for growth and learning.

"The only limit to our realization of tomorrow will be our doubts of today."
– Franklin D. Roosevelt

3. **Delayed Gratification: The Art of Patience and Vision**

a) **Understanding Delayed Gratification:**

- **The Architect of Long-Term Success:** The blueprint for building a legacy.

- **Patience for Long-Term Gain:** Delayed gratification involves resisting immediate rewards for the sake of long-term success. It requires the cultivation of patience, foresight, and vision.

"Success is not how high you have climbed, but how you make a positive difference to the world."
– Roy T. Bennett

- **Strategic Patience - Long-Term Vision:** Delayed gratification is the embodiment of strategic patience, the ability to envision long-term goals and withstand the allure of immediate rewards.

"Trees that are slow to grow bear the best fruit."
– Molière

- **Investing in the Future - Sacrificing the Immediate:** Delayed gratification is the sacrifice of immediate pleasures for the promise of greater rewards in the future. It's the understanding that true success is a journey, not a destination.

"Patience is bitter, but its fruit is sweet."
– Aristotle

b) **The Cuban Perspective on Delayed Gratification:**

- **Cuban Resilience and Vision:** The Cuban experience instilled in me the value of delayed gratification. The resilience of a community that endured hardships for the promise of a better future became a guiding light.

> "You may encounter many defeats, but you must not be defeated. It may be necessary to encounter the defeats, so you can know who you are, what you can rise from, how you can still come out of it."
> – Maya Angelou

• **The Triad in Harmony: A Symphony of Success:** As I reflect upon my journey as a Cuban refugee and the fusion of self-discipline, perseverance/resilience, and delayed gratification, the harmonious interplay of these principles becomes evident. The challenges faced as a young immigrant, the pursuit of education, the embrace of delayed gratification, and the cultivation of resilience have sculpted a narrative that resonates with the essence of unparalleled success.

c) **The Integration of the Cuban Triad:**

• **Self-Discipline, Perseverance, and Delayed Gratification:** The triad of self-discipline, perseverance/resilience, and delayed gratification integrates seamlessly. Self-discipline provides the structure, perseverance fuels the journey, and delayed gratification sustains the vision for unparalleled success.

4. Summary of the Cuban Triad for Unparalleled Success

a) **Reflection on the Journey:**

• **Celebrating Milestones:** Along the way, the celebration of small victories became a ritual—a reminder that success is not just a destination, but a series of meaningful moments woven into the fabric of the larger journey.

b) **The Universality of the Cuban Triad:**

• **A Blueprint for All:** While rooted in my journey, the Cuban triad is a blueprint for anyone striving for unparalleled success. It transcends cultural and geographical boundaries, offering timeless principles for achievement.

"Life doesn't get easier or more forgiving,
we get stronger and more resilient."
– Steve Maraboli

c) **Looking Forward:**

• **Continued Application:** As I continue on my journey, the Cuban triad remains a guiding force. The quest for self-discipline, resilience, and delayed gratification endures, creating a legacy not just for personal success but for the inspiration of others.

The triad of self-discipline, perseverance/resilience, and delayed gratification echoes as the underlying melody. From the shores of Cuba to the vast opportunities of the United States, this journey has been shaped by the disciplined pursuit of education, the unwavering resilience in the face of adversity, and the strategic patience to delay immediate rewards for the promise of a brighter future.

As I celebrate the small victories, learn from setbacks, and navigate the path of delayed gratification, I am reminded that success is not merely a destination but a continual journey.

> "The two most powerful warriors are patience and time."
> – Leo Tolstoy

The synergy of self-discipline, perseverance /resilience, and delayed gratification is not just a formula for success; it's the narrative of an unparalleled journey—one that continues to unfold with each note of the symphony.

In conclusion, the Cuban triad for unparalleled success is not just a reflection of my journey; it is an invitation for others to embark on their odyssey of self-discipline, perseverance, and delayed gratification. It's a testament to the idea that within the triad lies the power to overcome, endure, and ultimately triumph.

Chapter 15

TEDx Talk Delivered by Emilio M. Justo, MD

TEDxCherryCreekHS on August 12, 2023, in Parker, Colorado

YouTube Video Link:
https://youtu.be/OfOr-HP3QmA?si=FWifIx-ATlHnd6VY

Delayed Gratification: Your Superpower to Success

Do you practice delayed gratification?

When traveling around the world, I often find myself approached by people who recognize the University of Michigan logo on my clothes. Five years ago, while checking out of a hotel in Barcelona, Spain, on my way to a cruise ship, I was wearing my Michigan threads. The woman in line behind me asked if I was from Michigan. I replied, "No, I grew up in a small town in Indiana, but I attended college and medical school at U of M." "Where did you grow up in Indiana?" I replied, "Crown Point." Surprised, she said, "My husband grew up in Crown Point!" She shouted for her husband, who briskly came running up to us and said, "My name is John Kmetz." I was in total shock... turns out that John was one of my best friends in seventh grade, and I hadn't seen him in forty years! John and I embraced and quickly caught up on the last four decades in four short minutes as our families departed on the same cruise ship!

I wasn't always able to travel the world. I couldn't get all the things I wanted when I was young. Growing up as a teenager in Indiana, we had no money. My parents and I emigrated from communist Cuba when I was three, escaping a life of uncertainty for a better future. My father worked two full-time jobs, and my mother was going to college three hours away from home while attempting to speak a foreign language. I was sent 1,000 miles away to grow up with my grandparents while my parents re-established themselves in a new world. We didn't have a car, and I walked to school daily in the harsh winters of northwest Missouri. Some of my so-called "friends" made fun of our family for being "different" and having accents. Unlike many friends who had fancy vacations each summer or were gifted cars when turning sixteen, I couldn't have the immediate gratification everyone else got. As a freshman in high school, I wanted to play hockey for our high school team, but my parents could not afford the equipment. I felt cheated... I felt envious... and you know, even a little bitter.

We live in an era of instant gratification, where we expect immediate results and instant rewards. However, you can achieve your goals and dreams faster by embracing delayed gratification. When I accepted setting aside immediate gratification and instead focused on my studies and education to become a physician, I quickly learned that my life goals occurred much sooner. During college, I only had student loans and a few scholarships. I chose to live frugally and avoided spending on fancy meals but instead ate the meals in the dorms. I limited my partying and concerts. After graduating and starting my ophthalmology residency, earning a meager living, I chose to spend wisely and save. Within a few short years of working, I could travel the world, buy fancy cars, and, most importantly, financially support my parents, who sacrificed their lives for me.

Delayed gratification is the practice of resisting the temptation for immediate rewards and instead choosing to invest time and effort into long-term goals. One of the critical benefits of delayed gratification is the development of resilience, strengthening our ability to overcome obstacles, endure challenges, and persevere through setbacks. Delayed gratification allows us to gain clarity about our goals and aspirations. It forces us to reflect on what truly matters and identify the steps needed to achieve those goals. It teaches us to control our impulses and make conscious choices that serve our long-term interests. By delaying instant gratification, we become masters of our desires rather than slaves to our impulses. Delayed gratification teaches us the art of patience, allowing us to wait for the right opportunities and make thoughtful decisions, enabling us to embrace the journey rather than obsess over the destination.

One of the best-known studies that demonstrates the positive power of delayed gratification is the so-called "Stanford marshmallow experiment," conducted by psychologist Walter Mischel in the early 1970s. In the experiment, young children aged four to six were individually presented with a marshmallow or another treat of their choice. The researchers explained that they could eat the treat immediately, but if they waited for about fifteen minutes, the children would receive an additional treat as a reward. The children were left alone in the room, and their struggle to resist temptation was observed. The results were fascinating; some children couldn't resist the temptation and ate the treats right away, while others successfully delayed gratification to receive the second treat. Years later, follow-up longitudinal studies showed that the children who displayed greater self-control and delayed gratification performed better academically, had higher SAT scores, and exhibited better social and emotional skills in adolescence and adulthood.

Delaying gratification takes three simple steps:

First, clearly define your most important long-term goal. Reflect on what truly matters to you, write it down, and keep it as a visible reminder of your vision. Second, create a structured plan to achieve your goal. If necessary, break down your goal into smaller, more manageable steps. Assign realistic timelines to each milestone and chart your progress regularly. Third, practice mindful decision-making. When faced with choices that involve immediate rewards but may hinder your progress toward long-term goals, pause and consider the consequences. Embrace self-discipline and choose actions that align with your long-term vision.

I challenge you to step back from the immediate gratification culture and invest in your growth and potential. Remember, success is not an overnight phenomenon but a journey of consistent efforts and dedicated focus.

Next time you encounter a temptation, simply STOP and write it down. Do NOT act on it, but instead wait one week to let it sink into your subconscious. One week later, you can think about it again, but the temptation will be far less… this is how to learn to flex your delayed gratification muscle!

So, let's dare to be patient and persistent and let delayed gratification propel us toward accelerated achievements. Together, we can embrace our futures and make a long-lasting impact on ourselves and the world.

https://higher-order-thinking.com/wp-content/uploads/2018/09/cognitive_and_attentional_mechanisms_in_delay_of_gratification.pdf

Mischel, W., Ebbesen, E. B., & Zeiss, A. R. (1972). Cognitive and attentional mechanisms in delay of gratification. *Journal of Personality and Social Psychology, 21*(2), 204-218. https://doi.org/10.1037/h0032198

Made in the USA
Columbia, SC
30 October 2024

7ca04b5d-9287-472b-bcd8-9ddd36cf4c42R04